The Arrogance of Ignoranc

ISBN 978-1-7350607-1-2 (ebook)

ISBN 978-1-7350607-2-9 (hardback)

ISBN 978-1-7350607-0-5 (paperback)

Printed in USA

Library of Congress Control Number: 2020909320

WORLD OF WONDER
PUBLISHING

www.heidistampley.com

DEDICATION

This book is dedicated to my children. One of my greatest goals in life is to raise them to be faithful Christians and contributing members of society. My hope is that I instill values of humility and integrity that become the foundation of their successes and the reward of their pursuits. My prayer is that arrogance will never guide, drive, or overtake them and that through the attainment of knowledge coupled with understanding, they are led to greatness. May they blaze trails for generations to follow and eternity to applaud.

Love, Mom

FOREWORD

From the first time I met Heidi I knew she was a special woman. She had all the qualities I had ever prayed for. Since the day of our union I've learned of so many other qualities she had that I had not known prior. Her ability to gather tons of research, pull from her education as a registered nurse, take the information and sculpture those words in a very poetic nature is enlightening, educational and satisfying. Her first book "The Arrogance Of Ignorance" will transform your thoughts and your life if applied to daily living. This book is an easy read, but extremely powerful. Heidi's captivating manuscript will challenge you, motivate you and shift you into new heights. Heidi, congratulations on this heartfelt piece of literature. I'm extremely proud of you my love. You have truly WOWED me.

LOVE,

CONTENTS

ACKNOWLEDGMENTS

To my husband, best friend, and life partner, Micah, thank you for your tenacious love, support, and commitment to me. It has propelled me in so many ways. Your words of encouragement have empowered me to pursue every God-given passion with everything I have. I love you always.

With my deepest gratitude, I would like to thank my parents, Walita and Ronald Jones, for their steadfast love toward me in my life's journey. The patience they have shown me, and the wisdom they have imparted into me have been a life force as I journey through the corridors of life.

To everyone that believed in me, I thank you for your contribution to my dreams being fulfilled.

INTRODUCTION

Arrogance defined:

Ar•ro•gance: an attitude of superiority manifested in an <u>overbearing</u> manner or in <u>presumptuous</u> claims or assumptions.

The act or quality of having unwarranted pride and self-importance; haughtiness; an ugly often devastated or barely inhabitable place or area; something (as a way of life) that is spiritually and emotionally arid and unsatisfying.

The act or habit of <u>*arrogating*</u>, or making undue claims in an <u>*overbearing*</u> manner; that species of pride which consists in exorbitant claims of rank, dignity, estimation, or power, or which exalts the worth or importance of the person to an undue degree; proud contempt of others; lordliness; haughtiness; self-assumption; presumption. Closely related to the act of arrogating.

The idea for this book was born out of personal concern. Looking out into what is becoming of the world, it is difficult not to feel increasingly concerned. However, I am intrigued and passionate about how, in some way, I can shed light on some of the chaos. It is the purpose for my writing at this time.

Facing the truth about one's situation or self is not always comfortable or well-received. Most people simply can't look in the mirror and honestly handle the truth about who they are: the good, the bad, and the ugly. I wondered if this book might repel the very ones that it is meant to help. After much consideration and with great caution, I have written these words.

I am writing not as an expert with tons of scientific study or years of data or information, and in no way do I possess the vast knowledge of a scholar. I am clearly aware of my own deficiencies as my knowledge is being based on life experience and drawn from the psychology courses I took while attaining my degree. That said, this book is written from a layman's perspective as an innocent bystander looking out and making observations that may prove beneficial. My intention is simple: to bring light to truth and to help someone come out of the darkness of arrogant ignorance.

It is often said, "When we know better, we do better." However, the harsh reality is that many times we don't *want* to know better, because if we did, we would most definitely find a better and often more difficult way to behave or to live. To this point, the ancient proverb often holds as inherent truth:

Ignorance is bliss.

But when we examine the word, are they indeed true? Will *not* knowing lead to more pleasure in life? Does not knowing something make you powerful? I intensely disagree with that ancient solace that has given rise to indolent people who would rather forego knowledge and embrace oblivion.

This school of thought is the twisted mentality of those who have led countless human beings into captivity and depravity. Arrogance bred slavery and resulted in reproachable acts of human brutality. It caused humanity to carry out heinous acts of ignorance in the name of their own bliss upon people with the same biological makeup and the same intellectual capacity. Arrogance is truly the sanctuary of ignorance, and many times the cause for people believing things that are contrary to everything true and right. Delighting in ignorance has resulted in centuries of decay in humanity that still remains in recovery. The black hole of insignificance still haunts millions of the successors to cruel times in history caused by men's arrogance.

Ignorance is *not* bliss. Ignorance is reckless. Ignorance is self-serving. Ignorance is a menace to any society. The mantra of this manuscript will consistently be: *knowledge is power*. But *not* only that, knowledge is most definitive when coupled with humility. The paradox exists in finding a balance between advancing in acquired knowledge and sharing it with the world while not becoming a non-conforming know-it-all on the subject matter or life experience. You can feel you have received mastery in knowledge, but it will always be a work in progress, and you must not diminish those around you as your own knowledge is increasing.

Arrogance, the ever-present partner to ignorance, gives rise to the decay of the human spirit. Practicing it ultimately results in creating the emotional wasteland to be discussed in a later chapter. Arrogance will always be that horrid reflection of human imperfection whose putrefying effects degrade the very core of those who yield to it.

We've all seen egotism walk in a room and mandate that all eyes, ears, and thoughts become subject to its grandiose entrance. Yet there is arrogance too that isn't blatant, but nevertheless, no less unattractive. For example, we see the false humility that subtly drops the names of those with whom they have briefly rubbed shoulders.

We're all born with the need for significance and the desire to rise. The trouble comes when we don't know how to silence that voice that would rather see the insufficiency in others than to lose our need for relevance and significance. Were we born self-consumed and wanting our own way? A baby doesn't wake up one day concerned about anyone but himself or herself. Could it be that concern for others is a learned behavior only to be duplicated after demonstration?

When societies build cultures of self-indulgence with a lack of empathy, we see the desecration of those people. The fibers begin to tear, and we eventually don't like what the result looks like. Celebrating the rise of one at the expense of others is the characteristic of a communist regime destined to cave in upon itself. *All for one and one for one* thinking is destructive.

The behavior that is learned from it is to get yours and forget theirs; it's a dog-eat-dog world after all.

The truth is that arrogance many times is a representation of low self-esteem and the need to be recognized as significant. It may be that through the praise of others, there is a temporary false confidence in which one is able to indulge. People with true humility, on the contrary, are confident in who they are and don't have to parade their accomplishments or embellish their life stories. They are comfortable in their own skins.

Confidence and arrogance are both examples of character traits. One is a powerful tool that opens doors and creates loyal alliances. The other a flaw that divides and conquers, leaving a trail of innocent bystanders bruised by selfishness.

Arrogance doesn't take responsibility for who it hurts on the way to more vainglory. The expression of self is the sole driver of every decision, plan, and action. Arrogant fathers hurt their children with displays of rage that plants seeds of insolence. Children duplicate that arrogance by unknowingly seeking restitution for their grievances. Mothers erroneously model arrogant *sass* instead of *class* and create attitudinal disasters. They raise little girls who eventually transition into disastrous housewives or who become lonely souls who quickly drive away relationships.

It is not our plight to change the world, but it should be our desire to affect positive change at some level. The trial of our existence will always be to step outside of our own exaggerated world and chance trying on the shoes of another. How great the causes might be that we would take if we only were to forsake our own way for a day. The fulfillment we desperately seek can be realized when we embrace this concept and eschew arrogance.

It is my daily challenge to moderate my place in the world and to develop my strength by celebrating someone else's significance and his or her place in existence. It is through many pains to myself that this is accomplished. As Christians, this is the model that was put in place for us. I find rewards in this and encourage you to answer a similar challenge in your own life.

It is often a difficult exercise in finding the balance of self-esteem and self-worth without crossing the line into self-infatuation. Over-estimating your confidence on a subject matter, thought, or idea can easily put you into this quandary. Simply being rude and heartless in your expression to others because you simply don't care about their feelings can lead to rooted arrogance. It is the test of our wills to find something bigger than ourselves to believe in; to cultivate natures that nurture, celebrate; and to exaggerate efforts done for the good. Then and only then will we silence the ignorance that sustains our arrogance—a trait that will never be satisfied. It is a great feat to tame it!

So with all that said, let us all examine ourselves and embrace the broken mirror that is before us all. Hold up your reflection to the maxims that:

The truest characters of ignorance are vanity and pride and arrogance.

Samuel Butler

Nothing in all the world is more dangerous than sincere ignorance and conscientious stupidity.

Martin Luther King Jr.

Why

Why does humanity embrace arrogance? To everything under the sun, there is a root that comes from a seed. Human beings are formed from a seed. Things are formed based on the seed from whence they are growing. Strengths, weaknesses, mindsets, character, personality, etc. all come from seeds and roots.

It is important to address some of the contributors that feed the virus of arrogance that ruins so many lives every day.

Power and Wealth

Beauty and Youth

Status, Prestige, and Esteem

Intelligence, Enlightenment, and Education

Throughout history, almost every country which has collapsed upon itself has done so because of this otherwise seemingly harmless exercise of arrogance. The talisman of arrogance, indolence, and ignorance, is to be found in a single word, an authoritative imposture, which in these pages it will frequently be necessary to unveil as arrogance.

Man is arrogant in proportion to his ignorance. Man's natural tendency is to egotism. Man, in his infancy of knowledge, thinks that all creation was formed for him. For several ages, he saw in the countless worlds that sparkle through space like the bubbles of a shoreless ocean, only the petty candles, the household torches, that Providence has been pleased to light for no other purpose but to make the night more agreeable to man. Astronomy has corrected this delusion of human vanity: And man now reluctantly confesses that the stars are worlds, larger and more glorious than his own, and that the earth on which he crawls is a scarce, visible speck on the vast chart of creation. But in the small as in the vast, God is equally profuse in life. The traveler looks upon the tree and fancies its boughs were formed for his shelter in the summer sun or his fuel in the winter frosts. But in each leaf of these boughs, the Creator has made a world; it swarms with innumerable races. Each drop of water in yon moat is an orb more populous than a kingdom is of men.

E.B. Lytton

REALITY TV

n a culture where in the name of transparency, we've seen the evolution of a nation desperate for a shot at fame and fortune, I oftentimes ask myself the question that I would ask a failed Reality TV star. Was it worth it? When the cameras go off, and the charade is over, and no one cares anymore, then what? After they have run you into the mud and there is little hope for ever resurrecting your name and reputation, then what?

In the 21st century, if you haven't watched a reality show, it is probably because you don't watch television. Although this genre has been around for many years, in the last few years, we have seen the explosion of naked exposition into the personal lives of anyone who is willing to be filmed. In times past, the very thought of degrading family values and moral standards on public television would have been shunned and prohibited for the sake of protecting positive cultural imagery and preserving personal dignity.

Free speech and expression has always been an inalienable right in America. Twenty years ago, I don't think it could have been predicted that the course the culture would take a downward spiral into outright repulsion through Reality TV. We were still clinging to higher standards at that point.

All Reality TV has not been proven to be depraved, of course, but the shows that have made the most noise, seen the highest ratings, and caused the most devastation are the ones that have encouraged negativity and influenced culture most. This chapter is mostly directed in particular toward those type shows. At the end of the day, the end of a thing is greater than its beginning. Whether the end results in great detriment or great benefit is to be determined at the end. Why?

> **1**   *Reality Television frequently portrays a modified and highly influenced form of <u>reality</u>, at times utilizing <u>sensationalism</u> to attract <u>audience</u> viewers and increase <u>advertising revenue</u> profits. Participants are often placed in exotic locations or abnormal situations and are often persuaded to act in specific scripted ways by off-screen "story editors" or "segment <u>television producers</u>," with the portrayal of events and <u>speech</u> manipulated and contrived to create an <u>illusion</u> of reality through direction and <u>post-production</u> editing techniques.*

Reality TV description in Wikipedia.

More often than not, the path of the reality star begins with an approach with an offer to share personal stories or to bring to light a style of living that the world "needs" to see. Studies have now shown that the typical Reality TV star has the traits of narcissism before his or her fifteen minutes of fame begins. I am only reporting the facts. The promises of fame, fortune, exclusivity, and the rare chance of a lifetime are all lures to get people to sign on the dotted line. The pursuit of recognition by the world as important, relevant, special, and exclusive usually causes vulnerable individuals to fall into a downward path with arrogant manifestations. Tabloid exaggerations and blogger slander ultimately lead to the love of reality stars, and this love deserts them at the demise of every show. The end result has been consistently the same.

Time would not permit me to list the time after time scenario that plays out pretty predictably. At the root of the problem is *us*. We love to see other people's dysfunction and flaws. In a twisted way, it makes us feel better about ourselves. On the flip side, the often narcissistic individuals that play into our hands desperately need us to watch. They feed on our greed and our desire to root them on and to drop them when we get sick of their antics. The truth is we have a short attention span. In this century, we forget pretty quickly. How did we get here anyway?

There was a time when *Leave it to Beaver, The Waltons, Good Times,* and *The Brady Bunch* depicted standards to which we reached as families. The American dream to demonstrate wholesome family values was a cornerstone. People actually picked up some of their moral compass markers by tuning in every week and learning from the celebrity role models of the day. At the end of the show, there was positive resolution to conflicts and visions of hope that we, too, could be better. It was normal to protect, preserve, and live purposefully.

I'll never forget watching *The Cosby Show* every week and admiring the standards displayed and getting that heartwarming feeling of gratification (even if it was pretentious) that the world was good and people were, for the most part, striving to be better. Was that so wrong? To perceive that things could be good, that people could be genuine, and that humanity was not hopeless?

Many have suggested that those shows weren't real and that the families were fabrications of what things would be like in a perfect world. My response is, "What's wrong with that?" It gave us something to reach for and something to believe in. A real aspiration with substance was there, not the convoluted realities of today. So, are we better off being entertained by the sunken displays of humanity at its worst?

It would be remiss of me not to address one of the great reality success stories of our day: the rise of the Kardashian Empire. Many of the innocence has become victimized by trying to duplicate things they have seen on this show. It would be fair in my estimation to say that the Kardashians may very well be the most notorious reality family now and that may ever be for that matter. This group of personality types will go down in history as the mob of celebrity royalty.

The Kardashians have reached their goal and achieved great success in their objective of being on top of the world. It's hard to see anything beyond grossly exaggerated, but they have successfully capitalized on this. Unfortunately, we love it and hate it all at the same time. Everything, and I do mean everything, seems to be a publicity stunt. There is no life without photo ops and paparazzi. Sadly, the vanity of their famous existence has become the aspiration of so many in society.

What they didn't tell you: in the pursuit for constant recognition and cries for relevance, there is a price to pay. They are taken seriously to the degree that they can continue to entertain with more drama and antics. They dare not fall off; there is too much to lose. When someone signs up to be a reality television star, their first misconception is that it is a real portrait of their life. The truth of the matter is these shows are mostly scripted just like any other television show. It's about drama, and drama will sell a lot faster than your real life. Ultimately the goal is to find out how much drama can we get out of this? Plots and situations are presented and orchestrated. In many cases, scripts are even given so the plot can thicken and unfold in a dramatic way. The challenges presented are meant to cause fights, arguments, and chaos no matter who in *reality* gets hurt in the process.

The twisted inner craving to gossip and gloat in the problems and shortcomings of others is at the root of it all. Viewers develop gossip columns, criticize, judge, misjudge, laugh, and slander the reality stars for their need for fame, foolish behavior, and tactless transparency. The very things that ultimately bring them to deterioration fascinate us.

American magazine *Entertainment Weekly* wrote, "Do we watch reality television for precious insight into the human condition? Please. We watch for those awkward scenes that make us feel a smidgen better about our own little unfilmed lives. Media analyst Tom Alderman wrote, "There is a sub-set of Reality TV that can only be described as Shame TV because it uses humiliation as its core appeal.

The driving force behind the exploitation of innocence and the perversion of everything good, pure, and ethical is *money* and more money. The ugly head of greed seems to lead to broken families, suicidal fathers, and lost souls. The pain of emotional and mental anguish far outlasts the pain of losing material things.

Reality TV is mostly myth and fantasy. The players appear to have ideal lives. Many of the viewers find themselves trying to live their own lives through these "characters" and are trying to reach the perceived bar set by these individuals. The reality that begins to unfold off-screen is usually: broken marriages, unhealthy friendships, poor parent-child relations, vanity, bankruptcy, foreclosure, emptiness, and even suicide.

Though we would like to believe differently, many producers only care about money and ratings. As soon as these start failing, their shows will be the next to be axed while the producers move on to their next vulnerable victims.

Again, the million-dollar question at the end of the day is: Was it worth it? Unfortunately, depending on who you are, the answer will vary. Stuart Fischoff, a professor who founded the *Journal of Media Psychology*, said, "Shows such as Housewives have taken a unique place in American culture, but don't necessarily reflect society at large. These shows are really not average Americans anymore," he said. "You have a lot of exhibitionists and people who want to get into the biz who are sacrificing themselves." Fischoff said he was surprised that producers and networks hadn't developed a better support system for the former reality star akin to the advocacy group that now lobbies for child actors. "You're going to have all these people who are walking wounded," he said.

Another view can be seen from Ronald Richards, attorney for Russell Armstrong, suicide victim and former star of The Real *Housewives of Beverly Hills*, who said in an interview, "They prey on an addiction more powerful than Heroin or Oxycontin, which is the addiction of being famous." Richards doubts any support network will ever emerge. "I don't think there's a lot of sympathy for these people," he said.

Daniel Petrie Jr., former president of the Writers Guild of America West, an organization representing 9,000 Hollywood film and television writers, stated, "We look at Reality TV which is billed as unscripted, and we know it *is* scripted. We understand that shows don't want to call the writers actual writers because they want to maintain the illusion that it is reality and that stuff just happens."

The more people watch television and hence are exposed to these distortions of reality, the more they will come to view the real world as similar to the world portrayed on television and thus perceive a greater real-world incidence of the over-represented entities. The cultivation theory has been supported by a number of studies, although the connection is merely correlation and, therefore, subject to alternate explanations. Because television viewing is so common amongst Americans, it is nearly impossible to judge the impact that it has on viewers. Both the participants and experimenters are usually pre-exposed to so much television that it is hard to establish a base of comparison for an unaltered perceived reality. More often than not, the representations of social reality on television are not true to objective reality.

(O'Guinn, Shrum, 1997).

Our society has changed over the last decade. We're now much more of an ADHD, distractable, novelty-seeking, numb, over-stimulated, high tech society, and we're paying for it with our mental health. As one of my friends so eloquently says, 'you always gotta pay one way or another.' "Although our technology is beyond impressive and changing every day, we are suffering in another way—our divorce rates are up; our family unity is down; our emotional skills in dealing with anger, conflict, and anxiety are... not so good... and most importantly our ability to connect with each other authentically has been seriously challenged," says

Dr. Reef Karim.

So, now we come to the part when I propose a solution. The solution is more people finding themselves outside of reality television. Living your life vicariously through reality stars distorts your own reality. Eventually, if you continue to take too much of the Reality TV garbage in, you will become a product of your environment. Or you may seek out a way to get your own life on screen. Maybe it will work for you as it's just not that hard to be famous these days, the more over the top, the better. However, the price you may have to pay probably won't be worth it.

The fact is we are now at a crossroads. Some things will have to change. We will see change for the better when enough people get tired of the wasting away of our society. It will come when we reject the overly-prevalent corrosive media portraits of America and their outcomes.

A wonderful thing that we do see is people rising up with petitions against shows that demonstrate the worst examples of what models of womanhood should be. For example, there are a few brave ones who are not afraid to speak their mind and make a positive impact. At the very least, they are eager to get people talking. There will always be those outrageously ignorant stains on our television screen that are driven by nothing more than their own arrogant wishes. However, there is always hope for a balance with something better if someone would stand up and say something.

THE CHRISTIAN PERSPECTIVE

So with all this said, Christians are cautioned in the Word about the lust of the flesh, the lust of the eye, and the pride of life in 1 John 2:16. We are warned against falling prey to these temptations within our society and surroundings. It is very easy to become consumed with the systems of the world and those norms. Is it possible to live out the John 17 mandate of "being in the world but not of the world"? The enticement to follow the trends and duplicate the popular social role models has become a powerful draw.

As Christians, we are challenged to become counter-cultural and not simply sub-cultural. In other words, we cannot become subservient to the social and moral ideals that are diametrically opposed to the standards for Christian living just because it is the norm. We cannot simply put aside the values and principles we are given to live by in the Word of God because to voice such is just not popular. If we are genuine in our faith and sincere in our confession of such, then we have responsibilities as benefactors and disciples of that faith. Joining into the hype and becoming imitators of what secular Reality TV shows and their stars do is hypocritical and contrary to the faith we say is our own.

There is a new genre of Reality TV that has arisen, Christian Reality TV. At first glance, it seems to be counter-cultural, but with closer inspection, we see the infusion of Christian branding with humanism, the pride of life, and the lust of the eye to deceptively gain acceptance. On the one hand, there is nothing wrong with showing the lives of Christians and the norms of our everyday life experience. However, as Christians, we must be sure our motivations don't begin to lend themselves to greed, selfishness, arrogance, manipulation instead of piety and behaviors that are Christ-like. Taking up our cross is still at the forefront of the call of Christians. When we begin to lose this focus, we will begin the road to failing in what may have begun as a noble pursuit.

The world loves its own, and initially, producers may come along with Christian agendas that can produce great revenue for their companies. They may begin to wain thin if the drama doesn't ensue quickly and causes them to grow weary of positivity. At this point, decisions will come into play, and even some Christian stars just won't have the strength to deny the fame, fortune, and spotlight that can come with Reality TV stardom, even if it is destined to be short-lived.

> *None are more haughty than a commonplace person raised to power*. French *Proverb*

ATHLETES ON FIRE

You work hard, you play hard, and you make a lot of money. It's all good, right? Unfortunately, the statistics show a different picture.

> By the time they have been retired for two years, 78% of former NFL players have gone bankrupt or are under financial stress because of joblessness or divorce.

> Within five years of retirement, an estimated 60% of former NBA players are broke. (Torre, Pablo S., 2009)

Those are staggering numbers! How could this happen?

BLINDLY BRED ARROGANCE

Every boy growing up in America at some point or another typically has a dream. A dream to be a star who is shining and celebrated; to run out on the field or down the court to a screaming audience of fans and onlookers eager to see him make it to victory. The seed of arrogance is often born at an age when the word is not even understood and still difficult to explain. No one intended for it to be planted, but the harvest seems to produce the same product many times.

The course is simple. You sign your cute child up for Little League and Junior League teams. You go to the games and shout for your little athlete and hope that he or she always comes out on top. Many times you even insist your child comes out on top or else you demand harder work and more practice. Even if they feel like this is the ultimate punishment, as he or she really wanted to play video games or to play with a friend instead. The goal is the big leagues, the stadium, the arena, the lights, the camera, the action, and of course, courtside seats. You've convinced him or her and yourself that him making it to that ultimate sanctuary is possible; playing in a stadium or arena of tens of thousands someday in the future. And just maybe, you are right.

Before making it to the major leagues or professional level, an athlete has seen more of success than failure and more of victory than defeat. They have been the jock, the "it," the "one." The psyche at this point is usually one of entitlement and self-gratification. This is the way they were built. This is the way they were taught. Entitled to win and the feeling of being a winner oftentimes is at the root of the downward spiral that has followed so many greats. This is not the story for all players, but this book is about solutions, and we have a major problem with the outcomes of many athletes.

Arrogance is at the heart of the story of Gilbert Arenas and his guns. It's true of Ben Roethlisberger and his social life. It's what led to the scandal of Tiger Woods and his extramarital activities.

Arrogance is the key player in the stories of a whole new generation of athletes. We see it clearly in the heady sense of entitlement that has been instilled in some athletes from childhood.

You can blame it on the athlete and his or her parents and coaches. Blame it on our national addiction to sports, on the sports media, or on the sponsors. You can even blame it on the sports fan, but one thing is certain: it's not going away.

Woods, whose father had him hitting golf shots on national TV at age-2, and later proclaimed that his son was going to be the next Gandhi or Mandela, was speaking not only for himself, but, perhaps unwittingly, for some of his misbehaving millionaire peers as well when he said that he felt he was "entitled" to do the things he did. "I convinced myself that normal rules didn't apply," Earl Woods said. "I felt that I had worked hard my entire life and deserved to enjoy all the temptations around me. I felt I was entitled."

Entitlement is an extremely contagious disease in professional sports. Perhaps Roethlisberger caught it from Arenas, who caught it from Woods. We can trace it at least as far back as Babe Ruth, who was very lucky that there were no cameras around when he was chasing women through trains while traveling between big-league cities. (Brennan, C.,2010).

So one fine day you get a call from the coach that says an agent wants to meet the family. The agent wants to talk about making a career out of the very thing that has consumed your every thought and driven your every decision—becoming a professional athlete. Full of joy and amazement that you have come to this day, you find yourself overwhelmed with the possibilities and, of course, the money that awaits. You've worked so hard to get here.

It's a great time in the life of an athlete, and I'm sure that it is a time for celebration and parties. All of a sudden, the light is on them to shine even greater now and to not let us down. After all, "we" worked too hard for this too. All those practices, hot summer days at the field or court, money spent traveling to games and tournaments. Hey, *we* deserve this moment, and we've come too far to lose now.

It is not a stretch to project that these are the inner feelings of most athletes and their families, but for so many, this is only the beginning of an unfortunate end. Again, I dare not generalize this to be the story of *all* athletes. From the stories I have watched and heard, these are some of the thoughts that failed athletes have expressed. There are those that have taken a different course due to a level of character building which produced a type of athlete who is not entitled, nor arrogant.

The saga continues, and now it's time to take the big stage. The fans, groupies, and family are there, making sure you always feel like "King." Of course, there is nothing wrong with striving to be the best and determining to win. In everything in life, we should strive to be successful. The question that always must be answered is, "At what cost and what will we have to sacrifice?"

Professional athletes experience an enormous amount of pressure in their careers and lives. Both business and personal friendships and relationships all weigh in on the pressure athletes must carry. Friendships, even long term ones, often are rooted in the fact that they are stars. A friend that was a friend in the Little League days many times has experienced the perks of friendship with a star for years. Often athletes are unaware that the friendship's success is linked to the feeling their friends get from the connections to them. Not to mention, what happens to people when they have friends like Mike Tyson, who is said to have spent $50,000 on friends in one hour.

Unfortunately, marriages often also take a very difficult course. In the lonely world of stardom, an athlete feels the one that has been there with him before the majors will be there afterward, too. This is true for some, but for others, in tough times it's game over. The sad truth is that the marriage was solid when the career was solid. Going from being the girlfriend of the jock, then the wife of a star, to the wife of an ex-star apparently can be too much to handle for many. The finances aren't what they used to be, and honestly, they're just not used to this new lower standard of living. By common estimates among athletes and agents, the divorce rate for pro athletes ranges from 60% to 80%. (P. Torres 2009)

The arrogance often linked to being on top won't allow many professional athletes to live a life below their means. Preparing for the rainy days to come is often not on the agenda. If it were, they would possibly have resources to sustain them after the two to three seasons the average career will possibly see. The twin of arrogance; ignorance, or decisions made in ignorance always tends to be a culprit in the demise of a once-famous athlete.

THE IGNORANCE EXPOSED

The numbers of dollars wasted, and men and women who have failed to deal well with fame and money are staggering. This is not intended to embarrass as this information is public, but it is intended to bring light, so these mistakes don't keep being repeated in this industry.

Despite popular opinion, most professional athletes don't have the luxury of being millionaires, but this does not stop them from acting like they do. The rookies and veterans alike like to go out to the bars after the games to show off their status. Whether that means throwing away their paycheck for the week or not seems to be immaterial.

I learned something fascinating recently while watching a show that features several former professional athletes, including Andre Rison and others. I didn't know most of these guys are in a paycheck-to-paycheck lifestyle. In the NFL, getting paid this week is no guarantee you will be paid the following week, so it is important to be smart. Before you know it, the night at the restaurant when you had a $56,000 tab may have you on food stamps tomorrow. It's not a far-fetched scenario. Some of the most beloved ex-athletes are on public assistance or working for minimum wage to make ends meet. And as for the fans, well they've moved on.

So there are questions to be asked. What happened? Why is the scenario typical? What can be done to change it?

Most professional athletes in ignorance allow the following things to contribute to their demise.

LACK OF ACCOUNTABILITY AND BUSINESS ACUMEN

The truth is athletes are normally pretty headstrong and strong-willed. Frankly, most people close to them wouldn't dare tell them they were wrong or headed in the wrong direction for fear they would be cut off. Or maybe they just can't handle the truth. This lack of accountability usually causes arrogance to grow and feeds into a virus, which usually leads to significant problems.

In addition, many of the greatest athletes testify of their rise from humble beginnings—many of their lives being engulfed in poverty. The financial decisions made and lack of business savvy is often due to a lack of teaching and poor or little example of positive financial principles. The result is waste and lost. The strides that could be made in long term investing and saving with the amount of assets at their disposal is enormous.

Instead of reading the *Sports Illustrated* during free time, it may be time to pick up a book about finances or to invest in a subscription to *Fortune* or *Forbes* for reading enjoyment and personal development. It may not be their favorite type of reading, but a little goes a long way when you are ignorant on making money and keeping it and are extremely green on growing it. Knowledge is always power.

> A proverb that rings true: *A man's pride brings him low, but a man of lowly spirit gains honor. Proverbs 29:23*

▶ LAVISH LIVING

One thing that many athletes want to do when they sign the big deal is to go out and buy a big mansion, a lot of cars, and a great deal of things that they don't really need. It's almost as scripted as a road map. The feeling of wanting to live large often throws logic and long-term planning out the window. Hope for the best and plan for the worst is not the way they have been taught and programmed.

Win! Win! Win! This is the language that athletes have heard for several years at this point. So, the thought that it could be gone tomorrow is a far-fetched fantasy, and they usually will not believe it or face it! Soon the money is gone, the house is foreclosed on, and the bankruptcy attorney is called. It was good while it lasted, and now it's time to pay the piper for irrational decisions. It seems, according to the many testimonials, investing in car washes, clubs, and frivolous pipe dreams don't produce the returns of mutual funds and hedge fund accounts recommended by financial advisors.

According to the *Washington Post*, bankruptcy seems to strike professional athletes at an alarming rate. An article in *Sports Illustrated* reported a staggering 78 percent of NFL players and 60 percent of NBA players are bankrupt within two years of their retirement. They far exceed the bankruptcy rate of any other segment of society.

PARTYING HEARTY

Now that we are here...let's celebrate! Bring out the Chardonnay, Budweiser, and maybe a little marijuana for good measure. After all, it's just fun. It's all fun and games until there are consequences far greater than they are usually willing to pay.

A career and life can be shattered in an instance by a night of partying. Strip clubs and making it rain (a colloquialism for throwing money on strippers) seems to be one of the craziest trends amongst a growing number of athletes. The phrase, you are throwing money away, just got a new meaning.

FAMILY

They came to your games, paid your way, and have been there for you, so now you owe them. This is the feeling most athletes experience when they finally "ARRIVE" at the promised destination. The catch 22 is that if you give them everything, you are left with nothing, and when you have nothing, they don't have anything to give you.

So, faced with immense pressure, most athletes live in the now and forego thoughts of the future. Right now, I have millions, so I will spend it. This mindset, in hindsight, proves to be a significant factor in depression and even suicidal ideations following a retired or failed career.

 ## NEGATIVE INFLUENCES

Often the rough friends athletes had before the payout want to join the parade. Unable to drop the weights, many athletes bring them along for the ride. Frequently these friends influence athletes to do things their stature and privilege will not allow. When you're at a certain status, there are some places that you just should not go; and if you are seen there, there may be penalties you did not anticipate. Riding around with friends carrying guns and joints will soon catch up with you. Or how many times have we heard of a case of mistaken identity? Wrong place at the wrong time scenario? One wrong move and it's over.

 ## NAIVETY

A quote made famous by Forest Gump, "Stupid is as stupid does" probably sums it up best. Most professional athletes enter the world of sports with a fantasy that everyone loves them and has their best interests at heart. The truth soon is exposed, and they find out usually when it is too late, after their trust has been betrayed by those they believed in and trusted the most. Broken promises, bad deals with business partners, mismanagement by agents, and lies by friends and family have caused some of the biggest let downs.

The trouble is when you have always had things taken care of for you because you've been "King" for a while, that's your expectation. The tendency is to pass off a lot of the "little" details to other people and focus on what you've been trained to do and what you're good at doing. Although this is partially true, anytime you take your eye off "your ball" (your money and business), you will lose every time. Oprah, one of the greatest businesswomen in history, can teach us all something. I've heard Oprah still writes her own checks. Status, wealth, or influence didn't cause Oprah to take her eye off her ball.

It's not the norm, and it's certainly not the way it's done in the sport's world. The first thing you are told to do is get an agent. This person handles everything for you, and you leave it in their hands. This is a BIG MISTAKE. You just met the guy yesterday, and now he runs your life and controls your money. I don't think there is anything wrong with having an agent or financial advisor, but don't take your eye off the ball. You can learn from some of the examples mentioned previously.

When it comes to your money, the financial advisor, managers and agents have to be looked at under careful scrutiny. At the end of the day, everybody is trying to make a dollar out of fifteen cents. And you, my friend, are no exception. Big money means a big-ticket ride to the bank!

GIRLS, GIRLS, GIRLS

One thing that has always been public knowledge is the abundance of groupies waiting to snatch up the next big catch after the game. The groupies are waiting in the wings for their chance to be selected. I remember going to an MLB game in Miami. I remember seeing the groupies waiting to see if they would be selected. One athlete said groupies were everywhere and that they could literally take their pick. Very disturbing to watch, to say the least.

During an interview with a club employee, I learned that they had a list of women that they would text when an athlete came to the club. The list included about *7,000 women*. She referenced one instance when one of the top NBA players came to the club, and the text about this was sent out. She stated that within a short time, 2,000 women had shown up. Talk about big business and high stakes!

These ladies are not playing and are on the hunt for the next victim. Buyer beware. The problems start when they get pregnant, cry rape, or tell your wife. They may also give you a nasty bug that's hard or impossible to get rid of and impossible to explain.

You are in the big leagues, baby. There are people looking to bring you to ruin or submission intentionally. It's crazy if, after nine baby mommas, you still won't wrap it up. As if you will be able to afford all this child support in a few years. Unfortunately, the story is typical.

New York Jets cornerback, <u>Antonio Cromartie</u>, has fathered ten kids with eight different women in six states, including two with his current wife, Terricka Cason. He pays $3,500 a month in child support to each of his seven baby mommas, which amounts to $294,000 a year.

Others include NFL player Ray Lewis, who has six kids by four women; NFL Hall of Famer Marshall Faulk, who has fathered six children with four women; Calvin Murphy, 14 children from nine different women; and Evander Holyfield, who has nine children with six women, and so on, and so on.

THE CHRISTIAN PERSPECTIVE

Athletes are not exempt from the need for the right spiritual leadership and guidance. I strongly point out the word *right*. *Proverbs 15:22* admonishes us to seek counsel. Refuse good advice and watch your plans fail; take good counsel and watch them succeed. *Message Bible*

Athletes can be deterred from a lot of foolish mistakes and bad decisions through the use of counsel and spiritual leadership. However, there are those that have sought counsel, and the motives of the leaders were off base. Because of biased counsel, athletes have given millions of dollars to ministries, and when things went south, their counselors or religious leaders were nowhere to be found. Just as recommendations are given for agents and attorneys, seek counsel from leaders who want nothing from you but to see you live in a position as one of God's best. The search for this leader or pastor should start in Little League. When or if conditions warrant choosing to listen to different leadership, that difficult decision must be made if it means your future and sanity. Many athletes have lost life, love, and sanity because they lacked good counsel.

After writing this chapter, it may seem I have poured ice on the American dream. The opposite is true. The following quotes come to mind after writing this chapter:

To be conscious that you are ignorant is a great step to knowledge.

Benjamin Disraeli

Some choices we live not only once, but a thousand times over, remembering them for the rest of our lives.

Richard Bach

In a nutshell, if you've missed the mark and been getting it all wrong so far, all hope is not lost. Someone out there just has some decisions to make to change course. Parents of future athletes take your job seriously in building character, wisdom, and knowledge first and letting the game come after that.

BABY MOMMA DRAMA

So we've all heard the coined phrase "baby momma" and immediately connected it to a single mother and a deadbeat dad. This unfortunate combination has been on the rise in recent years. They have found a celebrated platform on the likes of *Maury and Jerry Springer, etc.* Many of the baby mommas of the world have seen their media worth go up as their values have gone down. The characteristics of being discreet and careful have been replaced with flamboyance and carelessness.

I find it troubling that for the sake of self-significance, silly women would use their innocent children as pawns for a seat on *Maury's* couch. It's touted as the noble cause of finding paternity, but the displays of desperate depravity throw out all supposed claims of pure motivations and dignity. Have they not considered the social labels and stereotypes placed on them about not knowing who their children's fathers are? By no means am I suggesting that these kids don't deserve to know who their fathers or rather sperm donors are. It is their right to be given this information. However, the means to an end should be considered more carefully. There are other options, including courts (although not as glamorous as TV) available to get to the truth.

Despite the seemingly compassionate attitude of Maury Povich towards his guests, "The Maury Show" is often accused by critics of exploiting dysfunctional families and minorities and for embracing and sensationalizing some of the worst stereotypes of American society and behavior. Although "The Maury Show" has a more serious tone and is less raunchy in nature, some critics denounce it as being even worse than other similar talk shows such as "The Jerry Springer Show" due to what is perceived as an insincere sympathy for the guests. Whitney Matheson wrote about the show in her USA Today column, "Povich's talk show is, without a doubt, the worst thing on television. Period. Don't be fooled by the pressed shirt and pleated khakis, Maury is miles further down the commode than Jerry Springer." In his 2005 book 100 People Who Are Screwing Up America, author Bernard Goldberg lists host Maury Povich at #31, writing, "I understand that many of you may find this hard to believe since Povich is supposed to be far more respectable. He's an ex-newsman, after all, turned talk-show host. But the fact is, Maury is just as smarmy as Jerry and also very much in the exploitation-of-losers business, making lots of money off people whose lives are in some form of chaos or another. And like Jerry, Maury does the usual staples of trash TV shows. He did one, for example, about women who are having sex with their daughter's boyfriends." Povich never attempts to contextualize any of his topics, and the show is devoid of any sort of social commentary.

Maury's show seemingly encourages guests to live pathological lifestyles with its endless procession of trampy unmarried mothers and men suspected of fathering many children out of wedlock, admonitions to inappropriate behavior "it's a man!" and celebrations of sexual infidelity.

Great care should be taken in the way these typically very weak-minded individuals are handled. Interviewers and journalists have repeatedly chastised Maury for his irresponsible exploitation of these fragile souls.

His response? He's a journalist reporting facts and giving people a platform to tell their stories. He has convinced himself in some twisted way that he is helping someone through the perpetuation of the most outrageous prostituting of young people and their children for ratings and self-centered returns. It's an arrogant, selfish abuse of humanity and ignorance of the generational effects it causes to society.

Maury would say, people *want* to see this. They enjoy watching. The truth is when people in the audience can sit back and laugh as they watch a 14-year-old girl brag about selling her body for a cheeseburger and having a pimp...we have sunk pretty low. This show should break our hearts, but instead, it has become a fun game and entertainment. When girls have paternity tests on four or five over-aged men, and no one says this is criminal behavior, we need some serious soul searching.

It didn't start this way. People used to cringe with broken hearts at the destitute and wayward destroying their lives and souls with these types of desperate acts for attention. So where did it all go wrong? It seems it crept in on us subtly.

The way I see it, we desensitize ourselves to the perils of others the more we sink into our own arrogance. As we see, the debased behavior of others deflects from the imperfections and struggles we have to overcome in our own life. The pain and problems of others begin to distract us from our own issues. We are able to live an elevated existence because, in our perception, we are not as bad off as they are.

Let's go deeper in our self-examination. Can we continue as a society to ignore the social ills that are driving us to a very dim future? Could the sex trafficking epidemic of young vulnerable girls be the result of our exploitation of these same girls on shows that portray them as sexually charged pieces of meat open to anything for a dollar and some attention?

Yes, it is true many of the young girls look like hopeless cases, but it is never the fault of children when they escape into worlds of darkness looking for light. We cannot blame them for desperately seeking someone to love and someone to love them; or for going to any extent and measure to obtain a place in the world. How can we place blame on them when they are dealing with a world that has horribly twisted the means by which they have gotten to a place of shame and degradation? So whose problem is it? There is a familiar African proverb that states:

It takes a village to raise a child.

Would we quietly sit back and watch a band of wolves attack a young lady and wait for someone else to speak up and call for help? Or would we act and cry out for help with the greatest of urgency? We are at that point. We all must find a way to speak out against injustice and offer some hope or voice in the midst of a world full of chaos. Is it possible to step outside of our self-consumed posture and care enough to do something? To do anything?

The human experience can come at a great cost for some. Like the savage beast, there are those that prey on the weak for their feeding and feed on the disadvantaged and dissociated. It is their nature to hunt and survive. Unfortunately, the inner thoughts, motivations, and actions of some pathetically narcissistic individuals carry the mentality of tearing to shreds the innocent for the sake of their own existence and survival. Survival of the fittest is at it's worst in these situations.

I have seen many women that get on this life course and never come off of that cycle. More and more children with different fathers and deficits in identity result in cycles of violence, poverty, illiteracy, drugs, and death. Those that have taken this path through ignorance must, at some point, accept their arrogance of self. In humility, they must face the fact that they didn't think through the consequences others would have to carry because of their actions. They weren't concerned about the children who would live in destitution and pain, including fatherlessness because of their reckless decisions. It is a stark truth, but a tough love. With the shifting in the economy, the welfare system will more than likely soon be unable to support arrogance. Those that have fed off the system in lieu of being gainfully employed will have a lot of challenges to face in the days to come. It is time to change.

I am not unsympathetic to the unemployment and underemployment trends currently facing the world. However, I have seen people come from absolutely nothing and rise above all circumstances and find the power to overcome obstacles. Albeit small steps forward will be taken with many steps backward on the way, there is a way out. It involves silencing ignorance and its friend arrogance.

Some have scrubbed floors and gathered cans with the dignity of knowing they had the power to feed their own children. Offering hands up has long-term benefits and is necessary for many to turn their situation around. Hand outs are temporary fixes that create a revolving door. When people are motivated to do more and be more and have the humility that goes with it, they will offer a hand up to someone on the course to self-sufficiency. Libraries are good places too for providing beginnings in quests for knowledge. You often see people bringing their children along while they search for jobs or materials to use in self-training.

THE CHRISTIAN PERSPECTIVE

We need more role models for baby mommas. In other words, we need more women to demonstrate honorable behavior. The type of modeling that causes them to be respected, valued, and what is called "marriage material" is badly needed. There is an attraction that men have to modest women for long term relationships. There is also an attraction men have for women that will be one night stands and motel check-ins. Media and modern culture is perpetuating temporary and free sexual expression but leaving out the consequences and the fact that it is unsustainable.

There is a silent but vivid movement to bring women into more loose living and to create more baby momma drama. The images that we see of a woman sleeping with various men during a season of our favorite tv series or having one-night stands on popular reality shows has validated socially irresponsible and ignorant behavior. These shows fail to show the broken children, sexually transmitted diseases, and depressive episodes associated with getting in and out of bed with multiple people.

There is little thought on the model that is being set for young women in search of relevance. Recently, I read that one such woman was being labeled a teen role model. I was appalled, outraged, and sad all at the same time.

Consider a major study that analyzed victimization data on over 11,000 individuals from three urban areas in New York, Florida, and Missouri. The researchers arrived at this startling conclusion: the proportion of single-parent households in a community predicts its rates of violent crime and burglary, but the community's poverty level does not. Neither poverty nor race seems to account very much for the crime rate, compared to the proportion of single-parent families.

Mental health problems also worsen when children are not raised by their mother and father. A study of the preschool children admitted to two New Orleans hospitals as psychiatric patients over a 34-month period found that nearly 80 percent came from fatherless homes.

A Canadian study of teenagers discharged from psychiatric hospitals found that only 16 percent were living with both parents when they were admitted. From nations as diverse as Finland and South Africa, a number of studies have reported that anywhere from 50 to 80 percent of psychiatric patients come from broken homes.

(Muehlenberg, B., 2010).

THE CHRISTIAN PERSPECTIVE

Christians must begin to fill a gap in society. The epidemic of fatherless children and baby mommas in some communities is beyond comprehension. Again, arrogance and bad attitudes have no place in this conversation. In order to help someone come out of this desperate cycle, you must be selfless, persistent, and committed. It is imperative that you be committed to correcting a faulty mindset in your church, community, and world.

Demonstrating the fruits of righteous living and godly pursuits will cause some women to pay attention. If you can only reach a few, it will be worth the experiment. Become the salt and light as spoken of in *Matthew 5:13-16. Eugene H. Peterson puts it like this in a commentary on Bible Gateway:*

Let me tell you why you are here. You're here to be salt-seasoning that brings out the God-flavors of this earth. If you lose your saltiness, how will people taste godliness? You've lost your usefulness and will end up in the garbage. 14-16

Here's another way to put it: You're here to be light, bringing out the God-colors in the world. God is not a secret to be kept. We're going public with this, as public as a city on a hill. If I make you light-bearers, you don't think I'm going to hide you under a bucket, do you? I'm putting you on a light stand. Now that I've put you there on a hilltop, on a light stand—shine! Keep open house; be generous with your lives. By opening up to others, you'll prompt people to open up with God, this generous Father in heaven.

> *A declining institution often experiences survival of the unfittest.* <u>John McCarthy</u>

> *In the kind of world we have today, transformation of humanity might well be our only real hope for survival.* Stainslav Grof

'll start this chapter with the following quotes which speak volumes on this subject.

"Be careful of your words, for they become your thoughts. Be careful of your thoughts, for they become your actions. Be careful of your actions, for they become your character. Be careful of your character, for it becomes your destiny."
Anonymous

"Profanity is the last refuge of the truly ignorant."
Anonymous

"The limits of my language mean the limits of my world."
Ludwig Wittgenstein

Profanity is a habit that usually bespeaks a vacuity of mind.
Clarence A. Barbour

Profanity is offensive. It destroys the dignity of speech. It is never necessary. It indicates a low order.
Arthur Growden

Profanity is the first stage of depravity.
Ernest C. Wareing

What follows will be a short excerpt of all my thoughts on this matter. According to the American Heritage

Dictionary, the definition of the root of the word *is to treat with irreverence, to put to an improper, unworthy, or degrading use, abuse*. Profanity then is defined as the use of abusive, vulgar, or irreverent language. I remember growing up the daughter of a preacher secretly pouring out my profanity on my siblings and my friends. Everyone thought it was a sign you were cool and relevant to be able to verbally articulate profanity eloquently. The truth of the matter was that it is often an outward sign of a degree of ignorance, often it is with great care and blatant arrogance that some work hard to display that they can use profanity better than anyone else.

On any given day, you can sit back and watch some of the popular award shows and television programs as they unsuccessfully bleep out vulgarities to cater to the advertisers. Recording artist, actors, etc. release their loose tongues on the world in disgusting releases of profanity spouted in pitiable arrogance. Foul-mouthed tirades that show a lack of vocabulary to express themselves. The fact is when you don't have enough adjectives in your bank to draw from, you are forced to expel the few words that you do "own."

I found a website called cusscontrol.com that I thought was humorous at first, but as I read more material in it, I thought it was powerfully relevant to what I wanted to say here. Here's a good place to end this. It's just as simple as this explanation by James O'Connor in cusscontrol.com:

SWEARING IMPOSES A PERSONAL PENALTY

It gives a bad impression
It makes you unpleasant to be with
It endangers your relationships

It's a tool for whiners and complainers

It reduces respect people have for you

It shows you don't have control

It's a sign of a bad attitude

It discloses a lack of character

It's immature

It reflects ignorance

It sets a bad example

SWEARING IS BAD FOR SOCIETY

It contributes to the decline of civility

It represents the dumbing down of America

It offends more people than you think

It makes others uncomfortable

It is disrespectful of others

It turns discussions into arguments

It can be a sign of hostility

It can lead to violence

SWEARING CORRUPTS THE ENGLISH LANGUAGE

It's abrasive, lazy language

It doesn't communicate clearly

It neglects more meaningful words

It lacks imagination

It has lost its effectiveness

THE CHRISTIAN PERSPECTIVE

I think that sums it up pretty good. And for the record, saying the same four or five curse words, every other word leads to very boring conversations. After a while, you just look foolish. You get so much further in life when you are actually saying something fruitful and productive.

The *Bible* gives us context on the type of conversation that we should have. *Ephesians* gives us useful examples and guidelines in judging the fruitfulness of our speech and conversation. *Ephesians 4:29: "Let no corrupt word proceed out of your mouth, but what is good for necessary edification, that it may impart grace to the hearers."*

Ephesians 5:4: "Let there be no filthiness nor foolish talk nor crude joking, which are out of place, but instead let there be thanksgiving."

Out of the abundance of the heart the mouth speaks. If our heart is full of vileness, then it is reflected through our tongue. This calls for a prayer that God create a clean heart within us and that the right spirit in us be renewed.

We cannot produce righteousness on our own; we need redemptive words to be empowered to live in righteousness. This still is not our own righteousness, but an imputed righteousness given by God because of our fallen nature. We need God's grace to overcome the works of the flesh. Cursing is one of those fleshly works.

The final scripture I'll share is *I Peter 3:10*, which counsels us about the reward of directing our tongues to good.

For He who would love life and see good days, let him refrain his tongue from evil and his lips from speaking deceit.

EDUCATION
CRISIS

A merica, we have a problem. But, it is not as if you didn't already know that. As I'm writing this, the dropout rate has become a serious social crisis in many parts of the country. It is a catastrophic trend. The culprits are kids that think they can make it in the fast-paced, technology-driven world without a basic education. There are also those that make it to graduation uneducated, pushed through the educational system to make room for others in overcrowded schools often run with substandard requirements.

It is alarming that more is not being done or said about this problem. The decline of the adequately educated in America and the rise in the well educated in other countries is significantly shifting. Today there are third world countries such as India and in Africa that are producing some of the smartest minds and creative geniuses in the world.

The questions I ask are: What happened to create this shift? What happened to halt the standard and automatic drive to get a good education and make something of yourself?

For the most part, innovation requires education. One cannot expect to make a mark in culture without the basic skills and tools a high school education affords you. Extreme measures must be taken to reverse misconceptions about this. At first glance, though, it looks like a hopeless situation to convince everyone that this is so

I will focus on the arrogance factor in relation to the dropout rate. Arrogance, in some measure, initiates and drives the first thoughts of quitting school for many students. It's an arrogant position to say things like, "They can't teach me anything;" "I don't need to go to school;" "I can get a GED and get a job;" or "I'm going to be famous." There may be a hint of fact in all these statements, but none of them are totally based on truth. Many students with this mindset will never rise to much beyond living with friends, family, or on the corner bumming money. It is essential that everyone strives to have a high school diploma that will qualify him or her at the very least for a job somewhere with a minimum wage.

The first problem to be addressed is the parents. Parents allowing kids to drop out of school is, in one word, ignorant. Parents are usually the blame for allowing kids that are defiant and arrogant to drop out of school. Consequences such as phones and Internet being taken away, cars being taken, and not funding money for expenses are sure ways to get things done your way. There is never an excuse for allowing kids to not get an education while living under the roof of their parents. Ultimately, the parents pay the price.

There are those situations when students just don't thrive in school settings for various reasons. In those cases, we now have virtual school options, many of which are free; viable homeschool options; and well-run alternative schools.

It's a dog-eat-dog world out there. Immigrants, both illegal and legal, have tapped into the limited job market that no longer cares if it's American made or produced. All employers and business owners seem to care about is getting the job done. There are those that are fortunate enough to find opportunities because of their talents, gifts, and skills. But, even for these lucky ones, there is still that nagging thought of not having anything to fall back on if the present situation falls through. It's a stressful position to live in.

As much as children and especially teenagers don't like it, they actually want positive reinforcements and accountability. They want to know that someone cares about them and their future. Make sure you are requiring accountability at all times.

Children need guidance, and parents who allow their kids to drop out of school without a fight are responsible for the outcomes. There are laws and means to assist you if you don't know what else to do. Homeschooling is also an option that many families are turning to in situations where their children are not thriving in a private or public school setting. Giving up on your child is *never* okay. By any means necessary, even juvenile detention, don't let them take a bad course in life without your intervention.

Arrogance and ignorance go hand-in-hand. I'll close this chapter with these observations. Life is full of uncertainty. Every day we wake up unsure of the course the day will take. The path chosen by a dropout makes things even tougher. Ignorant of the consequences of dropping out, millions every year in defiant arrogance walk away from a start in the right direction in the pursuit of immediate happiness. The old slogan *Stay in School* seems to have become a thing of the past. At least it's not as advocated as it used to be. Commercials and billboards have shifted into advertising other more lucrative themes.

When I was in 7th grade, I was given a poem to learn along with my classwork. My teacher, Ms. Cassandra Wilson, was passionate about her students and teaching them the value of their education. I remember a girl in my class that was seventeen-years-old. She had been in 7th grade for a long time. She had two children and was really in a tough spot. I am not sure if she ever graduated, but she was there unashamed and unconquered. The poem about education and learning was engraved on my heart, and I recalled it many times in my life. It brought me back to many realities and quickly reconciled me when I felt like quitting.

A CHRISTIAN FOR PERSPECTIVE

In the current times, it has become a great challenge to hold onto the Christian values taught at home while attending public school institutions. Schools are secular by nature and by virtue of the laws governing the separation of church and state. This state of affairs has caused many to become deeply discouraged by the eroded landscape into which schools have evolved. Sending your kids to school these days is no laughing or light matter. The foundations for Christian living at home are paramount if kids will be able to withstand the wiles of evil that has engulfed school campuses.

The hope is that parents will begin to take a greater stance in regard to their children's education. Leaving them to social networks, friends, and public school wares will lead to problems. Dropping out is only one destructive consequence in the cycle of many more to come if parents abdicate their responsibilities. Parents must be active in educational choices for their children.

I chose to begin homeschooling my children eleven years ago. My personal reason for doing so was to establish the values in them I saw as being essential for their success. There are those opponents of homeschool who have chosen to remain ignorant of the success rate and social benefits homeschooled children have. Many studies have quieted the claims about lack of socialization, and ultimately, it takes one conversation with the average homeschooled child to realize that this is not generally an issue. Socialization by the peers who are bad influences and secular humanistic views that are taught in traditional schools cause some of the trouble with the society. Socialization through means that establish foundations connected to Christian values has very positive effects upon children that last throughout their lives.

What do Harvard, Yale, MIT, Stanford, and Duke all have in common? In addition to being top-tier schools, they are just some of the colleges that actively recruit homeschoolers and offer them scholarships. What these colleges have discovered is that homeschoolers represent a very attractive talent pool: These students tend to be exceptionally bright, motivated, and mature. Far from being sheltered and shy (the typical stereotypes), homeschoolers' applications reflect students who have traveled, taken risks, and studied some pretty intense topics. In addition, they tend to have impressive reading lists and letters of recommendation. Most have volunteered, participated in sports, the arts, and in activities too numerous to mention. They are more than likely to have been dual-enrolled in both their homeschool and a community college and have numerous advanced placement (AP) and/or honors classes. Consequently, their GPA's and SAT or ACT scores tend to be well above average (Note to naysayers: If a student has stellar SAT or ACT scores and a community college GPA of 3.0-4.0, this proves that the parents did not fudge the student's transcript!).

Ivy-league colleges are not the only schools seeking homeschoolers. Public and private universities are jumping on the bandwagon, realizing what many Christian colleges have known all along: Homeschoolers not only enhance classroom discussions, they tend to get involved in campus life and student leadership, and they hold their own academically as well. Homeschooled musicians also tend to be some of the best, since they have much more time to devote to lessons, practice, and performances. Homeschoolers tend to have a strong sense of self since they've had more time to develop it and aren't influenced by negative peer pressure. (Staehle, D., 2012).

Homeschool is a viable and productive option for those that need alternatives. Dropping out is just not one of them. The COVID-19 pandemic has given a peek into some of the benefits of this option to those that would dare to continue.

The *Bible* teaches us in *Proverbs 22:6*, to "*train up our children in the way they should go, and when they grow up, they will not depart from those teachings.*" It is our duty as parents to make sure that we model our children the right way to the best of our ability. We must seek ways in which to hone our own education on subject matter that affects their development and foundation both spiritually and emotionally. We have a great responsibility entrusted to us. Our actions in child-rearing now could be the difference between a convicted felon and a college graduate.

> *That discipline which corrects the eagerness of worldly passions, which fortifies the heart with virtuous principles, which enlightens the mind with useful knowledge, and furnishes to it matter of enjoyment from within itself, is of more consequence to real felicity than all the provisions which we can make of the goods of fortune.* Robert Bridges

> *He who opens a school door, closes a prison.*
> Victor Hugo

"I'm going to be a star," countless millions have said. Popular kid shows have further perpetuated this with songs like "I want to be famous" as the theme to every pre-teens vision board. It sounds great. And it seems to be the life goal and career choice of so many in America in the 21st Century. From stage to pulpit, we have seen what stardom can do to the misguided. Could it be that popular shows like *American Idol, So You Think You Can Dance,* and *America's Got Talent, or your local talent search or pageant* have done more to harm than help? Before you drop the book and reject this statement, let me explain my point. I think it's great that Average Joe's from Podunk, USA, and Dreamers Alley are getting a shot at fame and fortune. They are willing to do anything to get their chance to be stars. The problem is we haven't found the balance or formula. Often we end up damaging more than aiding children on their journeys. Most of the winners don't even see the stardom they hoped for by winning.

Have we cascaded into being a society of Instagram and YouTube audition junkies hoping to be discovered and get our big chance? The old way of discovering talent has faded. With the emergence of technology, we have also been afforded opportunities at making progress at a much faster pace. This has indeed advanced the information age beyond our comprehension thirty years ago.

We most definitely should celebrate the strides we have made, but we should also be careful. It is astounding that little Bobby, with his extraordinary talent, can be seen by millions on YouTube or during his audition for American Idol. However, the side we fail to follow is the effects of the lack of character building many of these talented individuals are afforded prior to rising to fame and fortune.

Just a sidebar: I do believe in pursuing passion at some juncture in your life. This creates the life that is lived both in purpose and on purpose through the innate gifts given by God. I don't mean to advise not seeking a degree or job that can sustain you beyond mere passion, although that passionate dream maybe is the destiny of some. Many people discover that passion was where they found the greatest refuge and joy in life. Whatever that dream which excites you is, it should be added to your life's bucket list.

We all enjoy being entertained by cute kids and rising phenomenons. However, have we considered those that have fallen victim while we were being entertained? The list of those I could reference is exhausting. I spare further humiliation to those broken souls by not including them in this book. Many seem to have been lost forever, but there is always hope.

My two cents to parents with children pursuing stardom is to let them develop, grow, and be nurtured before throwing them to the wolves.

Money should not be the sole motive for pushing their pursuits. When the money doesn't come as expected, will motivation be lost? If you have a child in pursuit of this life, make sure they are ready for the harsh world of rejection and intimidation. Shed your pride and perhaps your own hidden desire for the spotlight and allow them to gradually experience the blows life brings. Having the weight of the world and media critics following your every move at too tender of an age can have debilitating results. One current example of this is Disney star, Demi Lovato. On top of the world, she was silently slipping into addiction and self-mutilating behaviors that will continue to follow her for the rest of her life. She has since been able to find help and seen a turn in her life, but she is a unique case amongst the thousands of child stars that have sadly been lost.

Recently, while watching some episodes from a season of the hit TV show *America's Got Talent*, I watched along with millions of others as rejection and defeat became the truth of hundreds of hopefuls. Two, in particular, struck me rather hard. One was a cute little six-year-old with the moves and voice of a young Michael Jackson. He had it all, and for a couple of weeks, we loved him. However, when the competition got tough, and the judge gave his harsh opinion that this talented youth just wasn't good enough, we all watched in devastation a boy who was crushed. Successfully holding back tears associated with his perceived failure, he stood strong like a little man. The fact is, he's not a little man. He doesn't possess the cognition to man up. I can only imagine the feeling of let down and despair that he must have experienced.

It didn't stop there, though. When he went home, he had to relive it at school, at church, and on the playground. As much as we'd like to think so, his sense of failure did not go away when he left the stage and was told to go back home. People had praised him all the way to the big stage, and they had placed a lot of hope in him and pressure on him to be successful. He was doing it for his fans, his friends, and his family, as well as for himself. At six-years-old that's a heavy load to carry. We didn't think that far ahead, though. We simply moved on to the next act.

You may say, "Disappointment is a part of life." This is true. However, there is a difference between disappointment and devastation. This is a man-made trauma for the majority of children, and too often, it cuts to the center of self-worth. The lasting effects can be seen on episodes of *48 Hours* and *Intervention.*

Shattering a dream in front of the whole world in the cold and heartless name of entertainment can sometimes be too much for anyone to handle. Sometimes the blow is softened for TV, but oftentimes the bruises of constant battering never fully heal. Recently, an 11-year-old girl hung herself after being voted off on a dance competition. This is an extreme scenario, but others may act out their pain in other ways.

Earnest preparation and great care should be taken in the perils of stardom while pushing toward dreams. Although I have focused on kids, this information doesn't just apply to children but is valid for adults as well. The decline into destitution can come just as quickly as the rise to stardom. No one, no matter how cute, adorable, or special, is exempt from the corruption that preys on those with great success and wealth.

The *Bible* speaks of the love of money being the root of all evil. It is indeed one of the great causes of falls and tragedies. The truth is on the path to happiness many never find it because of greed and discontentment. They are never satisfied. They never find contentment or gratification because the next level of success and wealth is sought so diligently that they fail to enjoy where they are. Unbeknownst to some, elevated sense of self-worth can be the greatest downfall of all.

Recently while traveling during a stop to the restroom at an Alabama gas station, I read these words:

Now and then, it's good to pause in our pursuit of happiness and just be happy.

Guillaume Apollinaire

Is it possible to do so? Father is climbing the corporate ladder and, at each level, missing the milestones of life that bring the greatest joy and lasting rewards. Desperate housewives nip and tuck without end until one day they wake up and realize the mess they have made of themselves. Frequently they look and feel more damaged than fixed and more incomplete than whole.

A CHRISTIAN PERSPECTIVE

So you want to be famous and have your name in lights? Well, it all boils down to motives. What are your motives for wanting fame? Are they vain ambitions of grandeur? *Proverbs 16:2* from *The Amplified Bible* says this, *"All the ways of a man are pure in his own eyes, but the Lord weighs the spirits (the thoughts and intents of the heart)."*

The heart is deceptive and will fool you every time. For the Christian, the only motivation for fame should be for the glorifying of God and bringing people to the name of Christ through your life's example. As spoken about in *2 Corinthians 3:2*, our lives are our greatest portrait of Christ to the world. We have a great platform for exalting the fame and name of Jesus Christ to the world. We must be cognizant of the responsibility as witnesses that we have and the impact that personal fame can wield.

The temptations that arise from the pursuit of fame are extremely challenging. It is often very rare to find anyone who has achieved a great fame and managed to authentically remain humble. The lure of self-pleasure in place of pleasing God has eroded the original intentions of many Christian fame seekers.

Although initial plans may have been accurately directed, many have met with an opposing fate. From recording artists to preachers, we have seen the monster of fame consume dreams, ministries, and lives. *Romans 12:3* speaks to correct this tendency, *"For by the grace (unmerited favor of God) given to me I warn everyone among you not to estimate and think of himself more highly than he ought [not to have an exaggerated opinion of his own importance], but to rate his ability with sober judgment, each according to the degree of faith apportioned by God to him."*

If the desire for fame is based on the feelings or thoughts of those challenged in humility in the first place, there is greater temptation to sink subtly into questionable actions. This is true, especially when there is a desire to maintain a place among those relevant in the world system. In other words, those who want to be in the "in" crowd of the who's who of celebrity society are in greater danger from their own arrogance. This is not to say that avoiding arrogance cannot be done in these circles, but it is to say the greatest of care has to be taken to be successful in defeating this malevolent giant.

Pop culture does not support purity, piety, and righteous living as the standard of the day. Therefore, the enticement of acceptance of your standards is the first ploy to bring you in. However, before long, there will be a backlash if acceptance of their standards is not complied with too. At that point, there are decisions to make because lifestyle changes may put you in a place where you must adapt to worldly standards or choose to move back to your previous residence. *Mark 8:36* would answer that dilemma with a question: *"What does it profit a man to gain the world and lose his soul?"* Taking up your cross is the price we signed up to pay as Christians. And believe me, you will most definitely be challenged on your beliefs and commitment.

Fame can be a great benefit and blessing. We should, however, not gain it through narcissistic pursuits and obsession. When fame is gained, it should happen because of God's approval and not ploys we try to forge on our own. When we seek to gain fame with our efforts, it is easy to slide into manipulation, contrition, arrogance, and deception to accomplish our goals, especially in the entertainment industry.

Focusing on doing things with pure motives and living to serve will cause you to become famous. Fame is not limited to lights, cameras, and action. Distinguished and celebrated are synonyms that carry great weight on biographies, history books, and the stuff great movies are made from too. If you never get the chance to be remembered for the red carpet gown or tuxedo you donned on Oscar night or Grammy night, don't fret. The books you may be mentioned in for your societal contributions or for the lives you changed through seeking greater good carry a lot more weight in the long run.

Fifteen minutes of fame has become fifteen seconds, in this culture...and anybody can get that; it's up for grabs on YouTube. If you're going to be famous, make it count for something and someone(s). Mother Theresa and Martin Luther King come to mind as examples of this concept.

> ❝
> *All true fame...is to be acquired only by noble deeds and high achievements and the establishment of a character founded upon the principles of truth, uprightness, and inflexible integrity.* Alexander H. Stephens
> ❞

> *Fame has also this great drawback, that if we pursue it, we must direct our lives so as to please the fancy of men.*
> Benedict de Spinoza

> *Fame is an elusive thing -- here today, gone tomorrow. The fickle, shallow mob raises its heroes to the pinnacle of approval today and hurls them into oblivion tomorrow at the slightest whim; cheers today, hisses tomorrow; utter forgetfulness in a few months.* Henry Miller

> *Fame is a vapor, popularity an accident, and riches take wings. Only one thing endures, and that is character.*
> Horace Greeley

> *Character is always lost when a high ideal is sacrificed on the altar of conformity and popularity.*
> Oscar Wilde

TEEN MANIA

We've all been there; in the *glory days* as they say. Some make it out intact. Some don't survive the unquenchable need to exploit, in reckless pursuit, the arrogance of their ignorance to the full extent possible. At 15, we see the scenario over and over for power's sake. In the space of 15 years, could it be possible the lessons of life, love, and happiness are discovered and wisdom developed? The obvious response would be, no. However, through timeless generations, this has been the test of household stability between parents and children. The battle of wits between parent and child met with much contention. Why? The answer is simple for within us all is the desire to be perceived as knowing more than we know to avoid being viewed as ignorant of any matter at hand. Unfortunately, the result is the opposite: the arrogance of ignorance shows up every time.

Rebellion, disobedience, and lying all have roots connected to arrogance. The exaggerated arrogance of knowing more than parents who have been down that road of life before causes so many children and teenagers in their ignorance to become victims of circumstance. How many countless teenage mothers in arrogant disregard go out and have unprotected sex with someone they think they are in love with, only to discover the love is lost nine months later?

Or what about the one that decided they would try the popular drug on the street, "Meth" for instance, just one time because they can handle it and there is no way they can get hooked after one hit. In their arrogance, they defy rational thinking, and in their ignorance of facts to the contrary, they end up a junkie always desperately in need of a fix. The culture, as it descends, is proliferating a segment of society that is growing up to be unemphatic, careless, lackadaisical, and more detached than we have ever seen. Fear of the consequences of life choices is becoming less of a factor in decision making. Kids are tattooing and piercing their faces with no thought on its effect on future pursuits because of arrogance that they don't need the system of employment to pay their bills. Living in the now is the only thought.

The problems are not helped when television shows like *Teen Mom* celebrate teenage drama, no matter how destructive it may be. The attention-seeking teen behavior becomes viewed as a new norm and is replicated by other teenagers. The boyfriend drama, tattoos, and piercing all glamorize and sensationalize teenage parenting and lewd behavior. Tabloids and entertainment media add to the hype with little consideration of the future repercussions. The arrogance of MTV and the like will not let it consider the children involved and the effects these volatile television displays have on society at large.

Beyond that, there is another aggressor to development teenagers are facing. The exponential rise in technology over the last ten years has given rise to artificial communication, emotion, and development. The following quoted texts explain this further:

Researchers are discovering that the gratification of getting and responding to text messages stimulates the pleasure center of the brain, causing an increase of dopamine, which may cause the addictive behavior.

The emotional issues are serious and varied. The very essence of being human consists of communication that occurs between humans in a very personal way, such as eye contact, body language, and listening skills, which includes discerning the tone of a voice, and learning to express one's emotions through the social skills of sharing in this very human way. Text messaging bypasses all the very vital elements of these very human forms of communication.

The Sacred Scriptures, especially the New Testament scriptures, highlight the power and beauty of table fellowship. We read of Jesus being involved in many such social settings. Jesus had table fellowship with sinners and was present at the wedding feast in Cana, and gave us the ultimate table fellowship in the Eucharist. Imagine His use of loving eye contact, the tone of his voice, and His embracing the leper! This very human and natural way of communication is being weakened and lost by addiction to texting.

Texting creates an artificial, introverted world in which people can hide from revealing themselves fully through placing texting as a barrier between themselves and the one with whom they are attempting to communicate. *(Karwacki, Francis. J, 2012)*

In an article on CNN.com writers, Gary Small and Gigi Vorgan wrote the following: "Their brains have become 'wired' to use their tech gadgets effectively in order to multi-task -- staying connected with friends, texting and searching online endlessly, often exposing their brains to shocking and sensational images and videos. Many people are desensitizing their neural circuits to the horrors they see, while not getting much, if any, off-line training in empathic skills. And the effects may even reach young people."

In a 2002 study published in Brain and Cognition, Robert McGivern and co-workers found that adolescents struggle with the ability to recognize another person's emotions. The teenage volunteers in their study had particular difficulty identifying specific emotions expressed by another person's face.

These young people were at an age when they are still developing the capacity for empathy, the ability to understand another person's emotional point of view. In many ways, the young teenage brain is non-empathic.

Scientists have even pinpointed a specific region of the brain that controls this tendency toward lack of empathy and selfishness. When making choices, young people use a brain network in their temporal lobes (underneath the temples), while older (and more empathic) people use the prefrontal cortex—a region that processes how our decisions affect others.

We are concerned that all this tech time interferes with young people's learning and development of basic empathy skills, such as maintaining eye contact or noticing subtle nonverbal cues during a conversation.

In a 2007 study of 197 students age 17 to 23 years old, participants were asked to quickly identify the emotional expression of a face as it rapidly morphed from neutral to an angry or happy face. Happy faces were identified faster than angry faces, but when the volunteers played a violent video game before the facial recognition task, they were much slower to recognize the happy facial expression.

Since middle-aged and older digital "immigrants" are catching up with these younger digital natives in the amounts of time they spend using technology, this empathy deficit may not be limited to just young adult and teenage brains. Empathy is learned, but it can be unlearned as well.

This problem is not exclusive to teenagers, but for the sake of this chapter, that will be the focus. Artificial communication has become our way of life, but is it killing the ability to have truthful expression? It seems that a trend is in place. Many teenagers have lost the ability to effectively communicate outside of a text message, email, or social networks like Instagram. They find themselves locked in a virtual world that is often not real. Many get trapped and simply never evolve out, carrying this problem into their marriages, jobs, or relationships and ruining things on the way.

A CHRISTIAN PERSPECTIVE

"Train up a child in the way he should go, and when he is old, he will not depart from it," says *Proverbs 22:6*. Teenagers are very elusive and not necessarily prone to volunteering any information. That being said, it is important for parents to ask questions until they get answers and not to accept the words of a text message as authentically fact or wholly representative of the truth. Simply accepting an answer that nothing is wrong when there are clear signs that something *is* wrong will cause you to miss key opportunities to save your children from some life-altering mistakes.

Being a parent that is always around my kids, it becomes a little easier to get into their heads, and I had started this practice from when my children were young. I've done it so much that now my kids are very curious every day to know how *I'm* doing and what's going on with *me*. Kids are great absorbers and are always learning strategies and picking up habits that they will carry into their lives.

Parents have the tendency sometimes to dismiss the cues that their kids give them. Sometimes more than we would like to admit, we may as parents adopt a know-it-all attitude that we are inclined to display to our children. If we were honest, we would say, "Mom and Dad know best *most* of the time, and the rest of the time, we're figuring it out."

Parents would be amazed at how children respond to humility and the door it opens to communication and relationship building. It's an art that is not commonly passed down. "Stay out of grown folks' conversation," I was always told. There is a time and place for everything, but sometimes kids need a grown folks' conversation to bring them to the reality of things and to help them develop and mature in wisdom and understanding. The truth is when we stop learning, we are dead. Many children have lost their way because they really believed their parents knew best, and unfortunately, the decisions they made were not the best for them.

I honor the role of parents and the place they have in shaping destinies and futures. However, may we all remember our place as creatures with a Creator who knows more than we do and can guide futures much better than we can. We are not sovereign, our role is limited, and it will never replace God's will for our kids.

May we be the moderator and not try to be the orchestrator of divine destiny. Teenagers need a lot of guidance and help with staying humble and learning the value of humility. It is important to find common ground with teenagers that prevents them from completely shutting you off and allows you to be an influencer whose voice carries more weight than the loud voices of peer pressure and negative influence. It is possible.

> *Use your youth so that you may have comfort to remember it when it has forsaken you, and not sigh and grieve at the account thereof.* Sir Walter Raleigh

n a culture where sagging pants is the status quo in culture, this subject matter may seem unnecessary to include in this book. But this book is about revealing truth and helping those that need ignorance and arrogance exposed to avoid ruining their lives. Somebody reading this will hopefully share this information with someone who needs it.

It seems there is so much arrogance that surrounds the wearing of sagging pants. Frankly, it is pretty disgusting and disturbing. It lacks class, and I can't seem to find any dignity displayed by exposing your underwear or buttocks and walking gap-legged to keep your pants from falling down. Nevertheless, there still remains a significant level of arrogance displayed with this behavior. Young men and women of different cultures, ages, and socioeconomic classes can be seen in any given mall, school, or street block with this ignorant display of the current culture.

Whose fault, though, is it that this has gotten so out of hand? Who can we blame for this charade in our public streets? The prison system is the answer. This trend began in the prison system to reduce the incidence of suicide by hanging by inmates.

In a recent bill that was passed based on the negative trend, the following was quoted by house staffers to provide a brief history of sagging pants in a bill analysis:

"Although no rigidly academic analysis of the history of 'sagging' has yet been conducted, it is commonly thought that 'sagging' originated in prisons where belts are not issued because they may be used to commit suicide or used as weapons. The lack of belts combined with loose, ill-fitting pants result in pants falling below the waist." (Tillman, Jodie, 2011). Another startling revelation that may get someone to thinking is considering the health risks associated with prolonged sagging, as reported by health experts and the NAMA.

According to posture and vitality expert Aaron Parnell, one of the biggest health problems is severe bad posture. Parnell, who treats over a dozen young people a year with problems directly related to wearing baggy pants or sagging pants without a belt, says many fail to realize is that to keep their pants from falling down, young people are forced to walk in an awkward manner. They rotate their legs inwardly at the knees and turn their feet outward to keep balance. This creates bad posture. He noted, walking this way can also lead to hip degeneration and low back problems. Further, rotating your legs like this every day can lead to life-long knee misalignments and bunions. A two-year study by the NAMA estimates that 75-82% of the men who wear saggy pants have some sort of sexual dysfunction. Because of the machismo associated with Hip Hop, gang, and urban culture, most men will keep the problem hidden. They mask their sexual inadequacy by displaying fits of anger and nihilistic behavior toward each other and toward women who they cannot please.

The study goes on to talk about the outcomes for young men who choose over-the-counter substitutes for Viagra and inadvertently cause their own high blood pressure and/or diabetes problems.

There is so much more that must be considered when decisions are made to follow the trends of the status quo. The problems that arise from being ignorant of your actions and arrogant in your response to knowledge can cause long term issues that are clearly seen in hindsight. The effects of long-term back problems, posture and gait trouble, and sexual dysfunction should be enough to serve as deterrents. Sagging pants surely cannot be worth the documented risks!

I believe mothers, fathers, grandmother, grandfathers, friends, and neighbor can help completely destroy this negative trend by exposing and educating those that are ignorant of these facts. It is often said ignorance is bliss. However, hopefully, bliss is not at the expense of health and dignity.

> *Ignorance and inconsideration are the two great causes of the ruin of mankind.* John Tillotson

> *It is impossible to make people understand their ignorance; for it requires knowledge to perceive it and therefore he that can perceive it hath it not.* Jeremy Taylor

HOUSEWIVES???

start this chapter with sincere concern and sorrow for the state to which many women have sunk in the 21st century. Without a doubt, there has always been a breed of women that have candidly demonstrated their low self-worth and possessed the arrogance that kept them enraptured in it. However, never before in history have we celebrated women who so openly parade their outrageous, vulgar, and simple-minded shenanigans on television and online in such an arrogantly ignorant way. It is painful to watch and take in the pitiful displays of buffoonery and raunchiness portrayed on some of the most-watched television shows of our time.

Let me put this disclaimer out before I continue. These are my words and opinions under my right to free expression. My opinions are my own, and I am sharing them in a spirit of inviting positive change.

Now back to my point. What is really going on? I can remember my first time watching an episode from one of the "Housewives" shows. I was curious about what all the madness was about and why there was so much conversation about these shows. To my surprise, I saw some of the most contemptuous, foul-mouthed ladies I had ever seen on Primetime television.

Television is the most powerful medium for transmitting societal values and ideals. Its ability to shift trends and to create paradigms has been seen for generations now. We eventually become a reflection of what we take in the most. It becomes our vision board. From children to adults, television can shape understanding and conversation. It is not long before we begin to react to life's challenges and situations in a subconscious mimicking of what we have seen on television. The more we watch, the more this becomes our reality. Studies have shown that people who faithfully watch shows that promote fear generally are very fearful of their surroundings. People who consistently watch shows that are very sexual in nature generally are more open with loose sexuality. People watching shows that celebrate foolish behavior before long will be engaged in similar behaviors. People frequently ingesting displays of perpetrating housewives will eventually start showing some of their behaviors. It will inevitably play out in dedicated viewers as their reality.

The funny thing is that most of the television wives are not wives at all. Many of them have never been married or soon divorced after becoming a part of these shows. The titles of these shows in themselves are deceptive. The role of a housewife would include caring for a husband and/or children generally.

In these pseudo-reality shows, the motives and objectives are clearly not geared at being models of the realities of real housewives. The integrity of their name and reputation, as well as the good name of their husbands and children, should also be considered beyond individual agendas for selfish pursuits. Frankly, how can they be a part of a show about wives and they are not wives at all?

So what is it? On most of these shows, all we see is reprehensible women acting like swine in sewage. Recently, while reading an entertainment news site, I ran across an article discussing one such woman. She was arrogantly sharing her sexual escapades with millions of listeners for more publicity while she was engaged to a professional athlete. She was not concerned about being discreet in revealing her sexual behavior. She just needed more awe factors to stay in the spotlight.

Is that what you would want to go down in online history about yourself? Because that's definitely as far as it goes. The Internet holds detailed accounts. A severely tarnished legacy of low self-respect is not one to cultivate.

I've read many stories of supposed "housewives." Many of them were the fiancée or girlfriend of a basketball player. Some of these women had been subsequently dumped at the altar or never made it there. Many times it was nothing but games. The ones who did get the ring were probably seen as *marriage material* as they say. Many of the athletes never intended to marry or commit to most of these women.

If you don't value yourself, no-one else will. If you will remain a sidekick and not demand commitment, then people will keep walking on you like a doormat. The old adage, "why buy the cow when the milk is free," rings true.

As for those that did manage to get a ring, many are either on their way to divorce or are newly divorced. It seems this is the story of many of these reality show women. It leaves a lot of questions that go unanswered, but most of it is based on arrogance. Ultimately, I believe when they begin to shoot the shows, narcissistic tendencies are strengthened. Traits that may have been hidden get successfully ignited.

Some of those traits are, having a nature that is argumentative, arrogant, conceited, vain, fretful, manipulative, and self-indulgent. These women are obsessed with appearance and the need for awe, adoration, and approval. *Bridezillas* should put enough fear in all bachelors to be careful in making their choices. Ladies, work on getting it together before you ruin someone's life and your own.

So the saga continues with new and more desperately outrageous shows like *Love and Hip Hop and the like*. These are pitiful realities the world could have lived without seeing on television. Folks on the shows are empty and self-consumed. They are also willing to do anything, no matter how low, to stay in the spotlight.

Here's what was missed: the children. They never get up and say, "I want my daughter to be a stripping, classless, sexually deviant, vulgarity-spitting drama queen," but this is the model they present. However, that's what is being fed to girls as the societal norm. Will there be a sufficient pool of chaste women fit to be wives in the next ten years? If we don't start intentionally injecting positive images and conduct into the minds and visuals of our girls, we are going to have a real problem. In fact, we already have a problem!

The problem today is that we are losing ourselves. The dignity and class associated with being a woman seem to be escaping our culture. Ladies, wake up! You are worth *more* than that. You *deserve* to be treated better than a sex symbol. If you want to be treated well, start with demanding respect by the way you present yourself to the world.

A CHRISTIAN PERSPECTIVE

Proverbs 3: 10 - 31 serves as the framework for the image women should pursue in being successful and godly wives.

Who can find a virtuous woman? For her price is far above rubies. The heart of her husband doth safely trust in her, so that he shall have no need of spoil. She will do him good and not evil all the days of her life. She seeketh wool, and flax, and: worketh willingly with her hands. She is like the merchants ships; she bringeth her food from afar. She riseth also while it is yet night, and giveth meat to her household, and a portion to her maidens. She considereth a field, and buyeth it: with the fruit of her hands she planteth a vineyard. She girdeth her loins with strength, and strengtheneth her arms. She perceiveth that her merchandise is good. her candle goeth not out by night. She layeth her hands to the spindle, and her hands hold the distaff. She stretcheth out her hand to the poor; yea, she reacheth forth her hands to the needy. She is not afraid of the snow for her household: for all her household are clothed with scarlet. She maketh herself coverings of tapestry; her clothing is silk and purple. Her husband is known in the gates, when he sitteth among the elders of the land. She maketh fine linen, and selleth it; and delivereth girdles unto the merchant. Strength and honour are her clothing; and she shall rejoice in time to come. She openeth her mouth with wisdom; and in her tongue is the law of kindness. She looketh well to the ways of her household, and eateth not the bread of idleness. Her children arise up, and call her blessed; her husband also, and he praiseth her. Many daughters have done virtuously, but thou excellest them all. Favour is deceitful, and beauty is vain; but a woman that feareth the Lord, she shall be praised. Give her of the fruit of her hands; and let her own works praise her in the gates. (Proverbs 31:10-31)

The rewards of being virtuous are more fulfilling than the consequences of being ratchet. How can we secure those rewards and model our behavior? By being:

1   Faithful – A Virtuous Woman is concerned about her eternal salvation and destination. She makes every effort to serve God in her attitude and actions. Her stance and relationship with God is paramount in her life, and she lives it out as such. (*Proverbs 31: 26, Proverbs 31: 29 – 31, Matthew 22: 37, John 14: 15, Psalm 119: 152*)

2   True Wives – Virtuous Women are helpful to their husbands and add to their husbands' lives. Husbands of virtuous women are known because of their wives, and are encouraged by them, pushed to excel and not torn down emotionally or spiritually. (*Proverbs 31: 11- 12, Proverbs 31: 23, Proverbs 31: 28, 1 Peter 3, Ephesians 5, Genesis2: 18*)

3   Respectable Mothers – A Virtuous Woman is caring, loving, and attentive to the disciplining of her children. She values their well-being and takes great care in instilling the Way of Christ into the fabric of their lives. (*Proverbs 31: 28, Proverbs 31: 26, Proverbs 22: 6, Deuteronomy 6, Luke 18: 16*)

4   Health Conscious – A Virtuous Woman cares for herself and her family. She makes sure everyone in her family is eating the right foods and is physically in good health. (*Proverbs 31: 14 – 15, Proverbs 31: 17, 1 Corinthians 6: 19, Genesis 1: 29, Daniel 1, Leviticus 11*)

5   Service - A Virtuous Woman has a heart eager to serve her family, children, and community. She is full of charity and seeks ways to help others. (*Proverbs 31: 12, Proverbs 31: 15, Proverbs 31: 20, 1 Corinthians 13: 13*)

6 Financially savvy - A Virtuous Woman is conscious of her spending and doesn't put the family in debt through frivolous spending. She is wise in her decisions concerning spending and bases decisions on the financial well-being of the family. (*Proverbs 31: 14, Proverbs 31: 16, Proverbs 31: 18, 1 Timothy 6: 10, Ephesians 5: 23, Deuteronomy 14: 22, Numbers 18: 26*)

7 Industrious – A Virtuous Woman is a hard worker and entrepreneurial. She uses ingenuity and makes wise business decisions. (*Proverbs 31: 13, Proverbs 31: 16, Proverbs 31: 24, Proverbs 31: 31, Philippians 2: 14*)

8 Homemaker and builder – A Virtuous Woman doesn't just have a house; she makes it a home that is welcoming and inviting. Her family loves to be at home because of the peace and comfort it provides. She also builds up her husband and children with kindness and gentleness. (*Proverbs 31: 15, Proverbs 31: 20 – 22, Proverbs 31: 27, Titus 2: 5, 1 Peter 4: 9, Hebrews 13: 2*)

9 Time - A Virtuous Woman is a good steward of her time. She is productive and conscious of the value of her time. She doesn't waste time with silly women or things. (*Proverbs 31: 13, Proverbs 31: 19, Proverbs 31: 27, Ecclesiastes 3, Proverbs 16: 9, Philippians 4:8*)

10 Beautiful – A Virtuous Woman is beautiful beyond external beauty. She possesses the inner beauty that exudes Christlikeness. It causes her to glow on the outside, and people are attracted to her grace. She is full of self-worth and class; beautifies her inner self with God's word; and takes care of her physical appearance so that it is pleasing to her husband or future husband. (*Proverbs 31: 10, Proverbs 31: 21-22; Proverbs 31: 24 -25; Isaiah 61: 10; 1 Timothy 2: 9; 1 Peter 3: 1 – 6*)

The ways of a virtuous woman are like a foreign language to the world's systems. Modeling after the patterns seen displayed by counterfeit housewives will only lead to divorce and distance you from a loving relationship. Don't be a victim and follow in the footsteps of foolish women. Commitment must be given to seriously practicing a walk in life that strives toward virtue in womanhood and marriage.

> *If one is not virtuous, he becomes vicious.*
> Christian Nevell Bovee

> *Character contributes to beauty. It fortifies a woman as her youth fades. A mode of conduct, a standard of courage, discipline, fortitude, and integrity can do a great deal to make a woman beautiful.* Jacqueline Bisset

> *A virtuous woman is a crown to her husband: but she that maketh ashamed is as rottenness in his bones. Proverbs 12:4*

GREED, SCAMS AND THE NARCISSIST

One of my favorite shows to watch and dissect is *American Greed*. It fascinates me to watch the tales of some of the most notorious white-collar criminals and examine how they scammed and ruined lives while they stole millions of dollars. The most consistent traits of these individuals are that they are charismatic, good looking, articulate, and well-groomed. Most of them present themselves as perfect businessmen. Their underlying nature is usually undetectable at first glance. These individuals hide their true selves from even those closest to them. *The Arrogant Chameleon Syndrome: A Behavioral Profile* offers a good look into the diabolical mind I describe.

A chameleon is a reptile that has the ability to change color to match its surroundings in order to avoid detection. White-collar criminals thrive on being able to avoid detection in order to carry out their fraud schemes; they have the ability, like a chameleon, to adapt to a given environment. What happens, then, when white-collar criminals attempt to become violent criminals? Do they have the ability, like the chameleon, to change their complexion to avoid detection? Or do they fail— exposing their true colors because their white-collar criminal skill set is inadequate when applied to violent criminal acts? The murder case data reveals certain behavioral traits that explain why red-collar criminals think their white-collar crime skill set can be duplicated as violent criminals. The behavioral traits are the effect of their psychopathic characteristics. (Perri, F., 2007).

Although psychopaths try to "blend in," the deficits in their psychopathic natures, i.e., grandiosity, poor impulsive controls, etc., hinder their ability to accurately foresee the consequences of their behavior. Psychopaths have difficulty projecting into the future, which is to say they have trouble understanding how their actions play out in (real) life, and they also have deficits in reflecting upon their past; "they are prisoners of the present." The red-collar criminal's inability to think through a plan that would take into account the potential risks of being caught, and the evidence trail left behind, is another hallmark of their behavior. (Meloy, 2000). The descriptive data is consistent with Dr. Hare's conclusion that because of these deficits, the red-collar criminal's self-perceived reality is distorted *(Hare, 1993).*

Put another way as Edelgard Wulfert, forensic psychologist and professor at the University of New York at Albany, stated, "A psychopath invents reality to conform to his needs" (Grondahl, 2006). The red-collar criminal's grandiose belief that having committed murder, he or she will somehow avoid detection, is proven false. In fact, the data reflects the exact opposite. The egocentrism characteristic of these chameleons produces an overconfident view of their ability to avoid detection; thus, they do not bother to conceal incriminating evidence.

These red collar criminals carry out their lies and scams with little or no remorse. Spending millions of dollars that is not theirs and taking the life savings of the innocent elderly while splurging it on cars and jewels is like a game to them. Some of their psychopathic characteristics are shallow emotions, stress tolerance, lacking empathy, cold-heartedness, lacking guilt, egocentricity, superficial charm, manipulativeness, irresponsibility, impulsivity, and antisocial behaviors such as parasitic lifestyle and criminality. Typically, these criminals create scams that will get them paid quickly. Many times they use their charm and charisma to win over gullible accomplices to join in their schemes.

The traps get deeper and deeper, and before they know it, they are consumed in an overwhelming mess of chaos and lies. Some of the cases result in suicide because they simply do not see a way out of the madness they have made. Driven by greed and arrogance, they destroy their lives and the lives of others.

Here are a few noteworthy examples of some of the top white-collar criminals:

Bernard Ebbers and WorldCom

Bernard Ebbers built WorldCom into the second-biggest long-distance telecommunications company in the U.S. in part through a series of acquisitions—including one-time industry stalwart MCI. That acquisition turned out to be an ill-fated move, however, and WorldCom's stock suffered. Ebbers allegedly tried to cover up the losses by cooking the books and artificially inflating stock prices. To make matters worse, Ebbers had borrowed $400 million from WorldCom to finance his other businesses.

All in all, the fraud amounted to about $11 billion. In September 2005, Ebbers was sentenced to 25 years in prison for his crimes.

Kenneth Lay, Jeffrey Skilling, and Enron

Energy giant Enron was the seventh-largest company in the country before its 2002 demise. Its fall seems like the stuff of fiction -- suspicious resignations, anonymous memos, shredding documents—but it turned out to be all too true.

The SEC [the Securities and Exchange Commission] eventually learned that Enron executives had hidden billions in debt and falsely represented revenue. Enron filed for bankruptcy by December 2001; thousands of employees lost their jobs and savings. In May 2006, Lay and Skilling were convicted on fraud and conspiracy charges. Lay died two months later, but Skilling received a $45 million fine and a 24-year prison sentence. (Mcgraft, J, 2012)

So is there any difference between white-collar and no-collar criminals (i.e. thugs)? Not really. The mafia and the gang bangers have similar roots to the crooked businessman and the scamming corporate executive. The end result of their crimes are the same—they destroy lives with little remorse. Their destinations are similar, too, as their crimes lead to death or prison.

Types of criminals are different, however, in some aspects. Thugs usually grow up in a different set of circumstances from white-collar criminals. Many of them come from impoverished homes or ones with limited resources. The opportunities for advancement in life for them are met with much opposition and struggle. Often times, as a result, these soon-to-be thugs fall into a life of crime and violence that is rooted in greed and arrogance. Desperately in need of acceptance and validation, they go to extreme measures to be the "big" man. Eventually, these individuals lose a sense of empathy and regret for their crimes against humanity. It becomes a game they play no differently than Monopoly.

We have all watched the news and seen the devastating stories of drug wars and greed. There is never a shortage of news reports on the blood baths of these criminals and the family members left in tears and agony on the scene. It has become so prevalent that we have become numb to it. We simply shake our heads as another one bites the dust.

All criminals are ignorant, as is demonstrated by their behavior. Their crimes show their arrogance. Yes, this is a general statement, but it is *true*. Arrogance has been defined as a sense of the grandiose and a state of being self-consumed. Criminals are motivated by selfish pursuits with a goal in mind; they have little care or concern for those that could be affected. If they were concerned, they wouldn't go through with their crimes. Something within them would stop them from destroying someone else's life or property.

The seed starts small. I personally believe when children are raised to be self-consumed, there is a door that opens and leads to self-indulgence and apathy. How many times have we seen the cutest of kids come into a room and within minutes turn into a character from a horror film? Screaming, raging, hitting, sliding on the floor, etc. in tantrums to have their way are common behaviors. We all watch in embarrassment for the parents. The result most often is that these children get their way to keep them quiet and not to cause further upset.

What you see as simple child tantrums in some cases are the doors to a lifetime of chaos and targeted manipulation. Many times these individuals will go to any extreme to have their own way. They've learned that negative behavior can get them positive results, and it seems to work for them.

From the spoiled kid who is overindulged, you can expect diminished respect for authority that wanes away from them altogether with time. They decide that the world should revolve around them and their needs. Everything should become subject to fulfilling the desires they have at that moment.

This seed for disaster starts so subtly that we may not notice it happening. It could begin at the Wal-mart when a child will not relent until he or she gets the longed-for toy. If that means a tantrum, yelling at, or hitting the parent, this is immaterial if it accomplishes the desired goal. It is a test of wills and a determination to win.

For years and years, children win in this struggle. Frustrated and weary parents fall victim to their manipulation. Many times parents fail to take their vested authority and demand obedience. They take the easy route and try to be a friend to their misbehaving child. This arrogance of winning his or her own way spills over into the child's adulthood, and he or she continues in negative behavior on a larger scale.

Lack of respect for authority, including law enforcement, bosses, and co-workers, can be seen as out of control individuals that go to great extremes. They must have their desired outcomes no matter who they have to step on in the process. They have learned to talk their way out of trouble and maneuver around obstacles to their prize.

Some of these individuals limit their shenanigans to timesheets and bookkeeping, but given the opportunity, they could easily move over the edge into bigger frauds. It's a familiar story the businessman that lies, steals, and manipulates his way to the top in order to have the prestige and financial means to buy himself the best of what life offers.

Then there is the no-collar criminal or thug who behaves similarly in that they too have a sense of entitlement. Their entitlement is usually rooted from a lack of respect for authority. If you look at the prison system today, it is full of men and women that lacked authority in their life or were taught not to respect it. This scenario strengthens the narcissistic personality traits that will create the thugs who do whatever they want to try to makes themselves happy.

Contrary to popular cultural standards now, fatherlessness and single-parent homes have consequences. Although these situations are seen as life as we know it, they have contributed to many of the social ills today. The prevalence of single-parent homes as a desirable alternative to child rearing has further desecrated the society. Even though this is a common reality in the current culture, it should not be advocated or promoted as a fruitful alternative to a home with a loving mother and father. Studies have repeatedly shown the best outcomes and opportunities chances for children to be within homes with both fathers and mothers as a parental unit. There are exceptions to these statistics, but probabilities are more in favor of dual parenting.

Many of petty criminals start out looking for validation and a sense of belonging because of deficits at home. They join groups of people who promise to give them a sense of family, power, and influence. Gangs gain access into the minds of the young because of their need for acceptance, approval, and responsibility. The gang gives them a sense of purpose. They have someone to report to who is concerned about their well-being. Although it may be twisted by the fact that the concern is related to building a crime network, it is no less accepted as family.

Sadly, this longing for a family will come at a cost. It starts off as petty misdemeanors, and before long turns into a life of crime and deterioration. Murder, thief, rape, drug addiction, disease, and death get written into life chapters. When it's all said and done, arrogance has taken over, and greed is in the fabric of everything they do. This is true no matter how ignorant these gang members are of the motivations driving their choices.

Greed is never satisfied. From the white-collar to the no-collar criminal, it is the same. Greed and arrogance ultimately take them down. With each successful scheme or deal, there is the desire for more. The greed drives them to the point of no return. It's insatiable, and once it has tasted the enticement of temptation, there is want for more. The distorted thrill of accomplishment and of being on top takes over; it is a feeling that takes more and more effort to keep.

Bottom line...blue-collar, white-collar, or no-collar criminals, you are eventually going to crash and burn. Here's a quote from the song, *Can I Live*, from the thug life-promoting rapper, Jay-Z. It sums up this mentality very well: *"I'd rather die enormous than live dormant--that's how we on it."*

A CHRISTIAN PERSPECTIVE

Christians are not exempt from the attraction to greed and scams. We can easily fall victim to the mindset of the common criminal in our drive toward *more*. There has been much opposition from the mainstream media to the preaching of what has been called the "prosperity gospel." Many popular ministers have been labeled as being a part of this so-called movement.

The line is drawn in the heart of each individual, and a true examination of motives shows us the truth. Is our desire for prosperity rooted in arrogance and the need to appear greater than others? Do we give to the poor and have compassion for those less fortunate than us? Are our own motivations for Christian living and service to gain gifts and rewards and not out of a heart of worship and admiration for God? What lows have we sunk to in order to gain prosperity?

We must be honest with ourselves. When these questions are answered and addressed from a Christian perspective, it should guide our decisions. Preachers can easily be tempted to manipulate people into giving certain offerings to meet selfish desires. This should be constantly shunned and avoided. There have been many ministers that have fallen prey to this temptation. After living a certain lifestyle and gaining the acceptance and approval of members and patrons, it is easy to develop a sense of entitlement. At this point, demanding it and even gaining financially by unethical means is tempting. It can only be resolved with submission to God. Many have faced public humiliation because they would not submit to the private humbling extended by the Holy Spirit.

We must all guard our hearts. *The Bible is clear in I Timothy 6: 10: "For the love of money is the root of all evil: which while some coveted after, they have erred from the faith, and pierced themselves through with many sorrows."*

To fall in love with money or to become obsessed with gaining wealth will consume your time and eventually your values. Being deceived, those that fall victim to an obsession with money will begin to become irrational and see everything as a blessing from God. Things that are even vile and are even against the witness of Christ will become acceptable because of blindness gained by greed.

Many Christians who acquired wealth by greed see it spiral into other areas of compromise. The circles of influence begin to widen, and many are just not strong enough to stand committed to their Christian witness. They eventually lose their sense of conviction and will go to the most desperate of extremes to gain, maintain, and achieve greater wealth, fame, adoration, and envy from others.

Money answers all things in the world. We need money to be able to live and thrive. However, we must be confident that in our pursuit of fortune, we don't lose our faith. As stated in *Mark 8:36: "For what shall it profit a man, if he shall gain the whole world, and lose his own soul?"*

The soul is defined as the mind, will, and intellect. Many have lost their minds, wills, and intellects while trying to gain world acclaim, fortune, and goods. The Christian should be in pursuit of the kingdom, which is righteousness, peace, and joy in the Holy Ghost, as described in *Romans 14:17*. This pursuit brings about godliness with contentment, which is a great gain as *I Timothy 6:6* advises us. When we seek first God's kingdom, here is our reward, according to *Matthew 6:33: "But seek ye first the kingdom of God, and his righteousness; and all these things shall be added unto you."*

Insatiability is a sign of worldliness and *not* of godliness. Our greatest satisfaction should be grounded and rooted in pleasing God and Him alone. We bring no glory to Him in pursuits with greedy motivations behind them. He looks at our hearts, and He knows its' intentions. We cannot deceive God by saying we want this or that to make Him shine.

God lives through us only when we are dead to our own desires. He cannot live in us freely without having *all* of being dedicated to Him. This process must be submitted to. It is a dangerous thing to act as His agent on the surface, but to truly be His enemy. God, being a righteous judge, will always cause darkness to come to light. We have His admonition in the Proverbs 4:23 Amplified version: *"Keep and guard your heart with all vigilance and above all that you guard, for out of it flow the springs of life."*

> *The world says: "You have needs -- satisfy them. You have as much right as the rich and the mighty. Don't hesitate to satisfy your needs; indeed, expand your needs and demand more." This is the worldly doctrine of today. And they believe that this is freedom. The result for the rich is isolation and suicide, for the poor, envy and murder.* Fyodor Dostoyevsky

ARROGANCE OF IGNORANCE

To everything under the sun, there is a root that comes from a seed. Human beings form from seed. Things are formed based on the seed that sprouted them. Strengths, weaknesses, mindsets, character, personality, etc., all begin from seeds and roots.

It's important to address the root causes of the virus arrogance that ruins so many lives every day.

Power and Wealth
Beauty and Youth
Status, Prestige, and Esteem
Intelligence, Enlightenment, and Education

Throughout history, almost every country which collapsed upon itself fell because of this otherwise *seemingly harmless* trait of arrogance. The talisman of arrogance, indolence, and ignorance, is to be found an authoritative imposture, which in these pages will be frequently necessary to unveil.

Man is arrogant in proportion to his ignorance. Man's natural tendency is to egotism, and in his infancy of knowledge, he thinks that all creation was formed for him. His hubris can know no bounds.

I thought about how to break down an explanation about the meaning of ignorance in a way anyone could understand. I thought ignorance would be analogous to a salad. Salads can be made up of all kinds of ingredients, depending on the tastes of the individual. Some people will have tomatoes and cucumbers, and others will have olives and peppers. There are no two salads that are made the same when you are given the opportunity to make your own at a salad bar. Even if the same ingredients are available to all, some will pick more or less of any given ingredient, and the result will, in some way, be different. The same is true of ignorance.

Ignorance is a mindset formed from lack of education, knowledge, or understanding of something or of a particular subject matter. Although ignorance, by definition, is in itself lacking something, it is at the same time full. Those with ignorant mindsets are full of disparities of fact, revelation, and common wisdom.

We have a salad, but a salad cannot be made without something to place it on, right? So we need a plate. The plate will be analogous to arrogance. For the sake of my explanation, we will say the plate is glass. The plate keeps the salad together and keeps it presentable, so arrogance always is presented as having it all together. The plate is firm and rigid, and so is arrogance. We can see straight through the plate as we can arrogance. Arrogance is a mindset formed out of entitlement, fear, and selfishness. The plate can stand alone, but it is not purposeful without something on top of it. The same is true with arrogance. Arrogance and ignorance go hand-and-hand.

Arrogance holds ignorance like a plate holds a salad. One day the plate drops. Just like a salad on a plate that you keep tossing, something is bound to fall off the plate. Arrogance will always fall. The fact is that the only way arrogance in a particular area is shattered is when it falls. Then the ingredients of the salad (or the ignorance) will be revealed. Then, and only then can the ignorance possibly be dispelled, and changes in mindset be made. To remain in a tossed salad state (ignorant), you must be on a plate of arrogance. The perplexity is that they must co-exist, which makes arrogance and ignorance as a duo, destructively powerful.

TO TWEET OR NOT TO TWEET

There are some things that should be left unsaid and unseen, but in today's social media society, it seems freedom of expression has gone to all-time lows. Opinions are our voice of expression. Everyone is born with the ability to form them. They can develop from life experiences, emotions, and from even just random thoughts. Our opinions are powerful, and they can shape mindsets and culture if we push them passionately enough. In a world full of agendas and those that will stop at nothing to make their agenda the status quo, we find social media to be a potent tool for this purpose.

Social media was formed to connect people via the Internet and to bring about a new form of sharing and communicating our local areas and to the world at large. If you haven't taken the plunge into social media, some would ask what planet you are living on. It is the all-seeing eye of the world.

There is nothing hidden on social media. It is a source and tool of exposition without boundaries for everything you are willing to divulge. The good, the bad, and the ugly infiltrate social media. With the social media revolution, we have seen the rise and fall of many. The detached persona of a Twitter or Facebook name has lent itself to cruelty and insensitivity beyond what we have seen prior to this era.

Recently, I was talking to my son about when I was in high school. When I told him that I didn't have a cell phone and that *YouTube* didn't exist, the look on his face was total shock and disbelief. He couldn't fathom that times had changed so drastically in such a short period of time. The more he talked about it, the more I realized just how much things had changed. Change is good, but when core values begin to fade in the name of change, we should start re-evaluating our course.

I think first it's important to define what communication is. This seems like a no-brainer, but unfortunately, the real definition is being lost each moment. Communication involves relaying thoughts, opinions, and ideas to another individual to express the intents and purposes in one's heart. So, where are we with doing this effectively today?

Not long ago, I read an article about a young lady who had been texting her mom from her dorm. Her online posts reflected a well-adjusted and happy college student. She had sent a host of smiley faces and cheery messages that gave the picture to her mother and others that she was doing great. However, in reality, that could not have been farther from the truth. She attempted suicide shortly after her last exchange.

This case is one example of millions of superficial communications that hide authentic inner feelings and emotions. In a world where image is everything, some lose their way and never relay the truth in their hearts, choosing instead to portray an image of perfection or happiness. There is a great demand for Twitter, Instagram, and Facebook messages. Many people thrive on the news feeds of others and attempt to compete for a life of greater substance than the next person. Lies and deception fill the profiles of desperate individuals hungry for acceptance and relevance.

When everything is done through a screen, we begin to lose touch with bona fide touching. In other words, the part of our brain that awakens to personal touch is not awake. Like robots, we simply go through the motions and stop caring about what we used to care about. Studies have found that college students, for example, are 40% less empathic than their peers of twenty to thirty years ago.

It has been concluded that social media and video games have created a generation of "me" individuals that have an increased propensity for tuning out the emotions or concerns of others. Many have subconsciously become devoid of the impulse to reach out to others in sincere concern without self-interest. When self-promotion consumes the greatest portion of one's time, there is little time to be concerned about anyone else. This lifestyle pattern eventually leads to even further detachment.

For many, the value of true friendship is reduced to a *like* on Facebook or a *follow* on Instagram. Friendship has become relative to the value that you add to one's network. Shallow engagement has left many hopeless and friendless in the midst of large networks of what are blithely termed "friends."

Many teenagers have become the greatest victims of the times we are living. It could start with parents taking a step back and maybe showing them what it means to really care about someone and how to be a friend. Leading by example is a positive step that parents may implement in a war against aloofness.

It is important for caring adults to help teenagers consumed with social media. Some teens, driven by arrogance and ignorance, totally lose sight of what is real and begin to create alter egos and artificial existences to keep up with others. Those that simply can't keep up often take drastic, irreversible measures after they have exhausted all their means to be seen, known, and heard to little avail.

At the very root of this problem is communication. The illusion that everything is okay has caused many to lose hope for intervention by those that love them. Offers for an exit and panic button are absent to the lost. Counterfeiting communication and sabotaging true expression has cost countless millions fulfilled lives and their pursuit of happiness.

As human beings, our only real method of connection is through *authentic* communication. Studies show that only 7% of communication is based on written or verbal word. An amazing *93%* is based on nonverbal body language. Indeed, it's only when we can hear a tone of voice or look into someone's eyes that we're able to know when "I'm fine" doesn't mean they're not fine at all...or when "I'm in" doesn't mean they've bought in at all.

This is where social media gets dicey. Awash in technology, anyone can hide behind the text, the e-mail, the Facebook post or the tweet, projecting any image they want and creating an illusion of their choosing. They can be whoever they want to be. And without the ability to receive nonverbal cues, their audiences are none the wiser.

This presents an unprecedented paradox. With all the powerful social technologies at our fingertips, we are more connected—and potentially more disconnected—than ever before.

Every relevant metric shows that we are interacting at breakneck speed and frequency through social media. But, are we really communicating? With 93% of our communication context stripped away, we are now attempting to forge relationships and make decisions based on phrases, abbreviations, snippets. [and] emoticons, which may or may not be accurate representations of the truth. (Tardanico, S., 2012).

The truth is that concurrent communication or communication that demands instant feedback is easier and cheaper. It doesn't cost as much intellectually or emotionally to send a text or to post a message on social media. Misspelled words and incorrect grammar are widely accepted as the norm. It is detached, and based, as the study mentioned only 7% of what real communication is. Are we creating a generation of individuals with a lack of real interpersonal and communication skills? My answer would be yes.

The reason I say this is because today, communication has become irresponsible. People hide behind their words on their computers far from the reach of individuals who could demand accountability before the words became a part of history. Once those words go out, you can't get them back. They are logged on some hard drive and artificial database for eternity. Ten years from now, those harsh words may still be out there, causing trouble in your life.

Even posts that have been deleted find their way into the endless space of the World Wide Web, and they can be used against you if necessary. There is no way to stop you before you release your inner feelings into the stratosphere of the unknown. Feelings, once sent out online, may change in the next five minutes. Unfortunately, after the damage has already been done, what has been posted cannot be taken back.

When we have a verbal conversation with someone, there are various aspects of the conversation that we intake subconsciously.

Tone, articulation, breathes, and fluctuations all affect the way a message is received. A mom, for instance, can say, "I love you" in a way that is totally detached and is received as such. Or she can say the same words with emotion, and they can melt the heart of a child.

Social media can be selfish and self-centered. While social media is supposed to be about connecting people 24/7 to those in their network, it has become more of an arrogant parade of emptiness and nothingness with little to no care for what's *really* going on with other people. If we were honest, would we find that social media can easily become more about self-preservation and promotion than connecting and relating to others? This may come as a blow, but maybe the truth hurts. Human beings are becoming merely profile pictures behind many computer screens in our world today.

Competition with everyone else's existence can also distract you from your own life. I often sit and observe people while at the gym or in the airport. I watch as people constantly check their Twitter feed and Facebook posts instead of engaging in meaningful conversations with those around them. Eager to check for new comments and responses to their posts, checking for retweets (or RTs) and dropping a note of insignificant value has closed the world to so many possibilities for *real* networking. Based on recent studies, it is a proven fact that people are more lonely and disconnected than they were before social media was available.

The hyperactive responsiveness of those hungry for media attention causes some to post messages at speeds too quick to be digested. If they were to ask those that they are trying to reach if they saw their post, many times, the resounding response would be, "*No!*" Alas, we couldn't help but miss messages in the random flood of feeds too frequent to digest or process, let alone remember.

Eventually, over-eager people in social media get blocked, unfriended, or ignored so much that they go into a deeper hole. They are then in need of taking more drastic measures to be noticed. There is no shortage of this in the case of celebrities. Some of whom go to dire straits to stay the subject of conversation.

Whether positive or negative, contrived or authentic, we eventually just tune them out, or talk about our annoyance with their rants.

A Word to Husbands and Wives

Marriages too have also fallen victim to the wares of social media. We hear stories of husbands posting messages about how great their love is for their wife and shortly after killing her. Or wives sending posts to their husbands while secretly posting to their lover as well.

 Some would say it's cute, and they aren't ashamed to share their love with the world. However, I think that feelings mean more when they are expressed verbally, and actions speak louder than words. It may be a choice of sharing loving feelings so that the world can see them. I'm not saying it can't be authentic because I believe that it can; however, it should be purely motivated. I'm all for celebrating love.

Husbands and wives should never hide behind social media to communicate. By any means necessary, they should find a way to speak words face-to-face, in spite of all the nuisances, and because of all the inflections and emotions that a conversation gives. If your intention is to demonstrate your love for others to see, at least make sure it is authentic! It is easy to be driven by arrogance only wanting others to see and celebrate your love with words of praise but ultimately to envy it.

A WORD TO PARENTS

I can imagine it would be hard for teenagers to say goodnight to friends on Instagram or chatters on Snapchat. In their minds, people are waiting on their next post. The thoughts ring through their heads as they sit there and wait for comments, wait for information, and peer into the lives of those that are less friend and more like noisy neighbors. Often they are like you, and only want a look into your world in search of gossip topics. The result may be little to no sleep or restless sleep, thinking about what just happened on your social network. Ultimately addicted and consumed, they may prefer to engage in socializing online rather than in learning at school. Conversely, all the socializing online may affect what happens at school and result in problems like bullying. Letting everyone into their sphere and world sometimes has devastating effects. Many find this out the hard way.

I want to sidebar into a very serious topic that can tag this subject matter: *cyberbullying*. The frightening scenarios and stories we see in the news are reason for great alarm! Cyberbullies hide behind their computers and seek to create nightmares through online harassment. Most of the time, these individuals are full of dysfunction and looking for ways to ruin other peoples' lives. They find infinite pleasure in making other people go through living hell. Most of the time, cyberbullies are blinded by their own ignorance. They frustrate and intimidate others, and this heightens their feelings of arrogance.

These people are empty and lonely. Typically cyberbullies have dealt with some form of rejection in their own life experience that has caused them to project their intimidation on others. They are extremely dangerous, especially in today's society that promotes social media and makes it easy for them to torment others electronically.

Cyber-bullying takes on many different forms, according to Amani. There is "flaming," which are online fights using aggressive language. Harassment is sending nasty, mean, and insulting messages. Denigration is "dissing" someone online by sending or posting gossip and rumors. Impersonation is assuming the identity of someone to purposely damage the person's reputation. "Outing" is sharing secrets to other people, while "trickery" involves talking someone into revealing secrets and then sharing them online. (Tat, J., 2010)

Parents really have to get a clue. It's so easy to turn off the lights at night and leave your children to themselves. Not to mention all the time they spend online chatting, tweeting, and texting during the day. In spite of how great you think your children are, do not fail to monitor their time. Don't let them carry on without knowing *how* they are carrying on. Are they involved in behavior online that could ruin their lives or result in physical harm?

The fact is that there is a lot of carry-over from cyberspace to real life. Bullies online usually don't stop there. They like to take it to the next level. Unfortunately, many kids can't handle the pressure and end up extremely depressed, suicidal, or dead. Reading through the online news publications, you can read many stories of cyberbullying.

According to the Centers for Disease Control and Prevention, more than 15 percent of teens consider suicide due to bullying in school. Half of those students attempt it. Each day, 160,000 students ask to be sent home or skip class to avoid being bullied. This issue has become such a serious problem that the government has launched campaigns to stop it.

The reality is that bullying has always existed in school. Now it has extended beyond the school, and kids can't get away from it. Instagram and other social media sites have given rise to a new playground for bullies on a mission to destroy lives.

You must find time to get in your kids' business and to know the pressures and trials they are going through. You can't sit back ignorantly on your own social network while right under your roof, your child may be under attack and bullied to the point of considering suicide.

So with all this said, how do we find balance in the new age of technology? How can we maintain relationships and find fulfillment in a system mimicking robotic communication? There is a way. The first step is to step out of the virtual world more than you are in it. If you find yourself ruled by your feeds, then you are in need of an intervention before you lose every relationship you have. You cannot be consumed with a virtual world and maintain a vibrant human connection. It will fail. Arrogance causes us to have an elevated sense of importance. Social media many times heightened this to an extreme level.

Finding purpose and meaning in giving to something for a greater good; feeding and nurturing without selfish ambition are noble real-world aspirations. Parents, that set of goals should start with your children. Husbands and wives, that agenda should start within your marriage. Pastors, that plan should include your congregation. Teachers, that list should include activities for your students. Coaches, that list should include your team as participants. Executive, that community action would include your employees. Business owners, how can doing unselfish good for others be included in your business plans?

By the time you feed all the things that mean the most to your real world, you will have little time to share pieces of yourself with the hundreds of artificial friends in your social networks. The sooner you understand this concept, the more relevant your life will become. Relevancy has *nothing* to do with how many friends or followers you have on social networks.

The measure of your relevance will be how much you came out of your own arrogance to bring about a greater good for someone else. Focusing on the things that matter in life and releasing some of the insignificant details will make more room in your life for greater fulfillment. For example, the sandwich you ate at Subway just isn't that important in the bigger picture.

By the way, get a photo album and print some of those pictures you have on Facebook or Instagram. As unfailing as we think technology is, one day, it may crash, and all those great memories you posted would be lost. Hold on to the tangible tighter than the virtual. Call it My (real) space.

> *Words mean more than what is set down on paper.*
> *It takes the human voice to infuse them with deeper meaning.*
> Maya Angelou

> *Words, like nature, half reveal and half conceal*
> *the soul within.* Alfred Lord Tennyson

PROMISCUITY

From Arnold Schwarzenegger to John Edwards, we have seen the rise and fall of many greats because of sexual arrogance. The dictionary definition of promiscuity is *the casual or thoughtless joining of individuals without regard to reason*.

So what is sexual arrogance? I came across this terminology while doing research for this book. It is the idea of sexual entitlement and limited restraint in obtaining it or having it your way. I wanted to write this chapter with as little restraint as possible and to be vividly candid.

A study set to be published in <u>Psychological Science</u> found that the higher men—or women—rose in a business hierarchy, the more likely they were to consider or commit adultery. With power comes both opportunity and confidence, the authors argue, and with confidence comes a sense of sexual entitlement. If fame and power make sex more constantly available, the evolutionary biologists explain, it may weaken the mechanisms of self-restraint and erode the layers of socialization that we impose on teenage boys and hope they eventually internalize.

"When men have more opportunity, they tend to act on that opportunity," says psychologist Mark Held, a private practitioner in the Denver area who specializes in male sexuality and the problems of overachievers. "The challenge becomes developing ways to control the

impulses so you don't get yourself into self-defeating situations." (Gibbs, N., 2011).

This book is about the arrogance of ignorance, so it is imperative that I make my point. There has always been a negative undertone associated with those that sleep around, especially for women. The terms "loose woman" or "slut" don't carry any context of respectability or class. No matter how you try to dress it up, this type of reputation is always looked down on. So, why do we have an increasing perpetuation of the image of casual sex in our culture? The answer is arrogance and ignorance.

The media and music industry in the last twenty years has increased its presentation and desensitization of society as it relates to casual sexual relationships. It is normal these days to watch a movie or TV show where the main characters have sex or intimacy with multiple partners in the space of thirty minutes or two hours. The repeated portrayal of free sex gives the impression of this being a normal human experience. As a result, people have lost touch with reality and the power of commitment and monogamy. Strong emotional attachment and love are taken out of the equation and replaced only with the one-sided emotion of attraction. In other words, if you like what you see, you can have it or go after it.

Lust drives many to do the unthinkable as a manifestation of their unrestrained arrogance. Others act out their feelings with little thought of the consequences or results of their behavior. Lewd photo leaks show deep-seated arrogance. The inability to see any potential for consequences will cause people to do some of the craziest things. It leaves us all wondering why they would risk it all.

Recently, I read a story of a person who was engaging in sexual activity while married with several people in spite of knowing he was HIV positive.

His feeling of grandeur was so strong that it allowed him to dismiss the value of another's life in order to fulfill his own selfish desires.

The effects of promiscuous behavior roll over once married as well. Statistics show a direct correlation to the rise in promiscuity and divorce. Some of the factors cited are the fact that promiscuity causes problems with making emotional commitments and increases the likelihood of divorce. It should also be noted that virgins only have a 5% divorce rate. This is compared to the 50% divorce rate among the rest of the population.

I read another article in which a popular actress said she did not believe in marriage because she had never seen a successful one since she had grown up in Los Angeles. It is a sad notion. In Hollywood, where sexual freedom, adultery, and lewdness are celebrated, marriage is most definitely seen as a challenge. The climate just doesn't seem conducive for solid relationships. It is almost an entertainment industry standard to divorce. The actress in the article had resolved that a marriage commitment was probably not an option because of the cultural landscape of her surroundings. Therefore to her *sons*, the picture that she would paint is that marriages don't work.

Society is on the fast track to a total loss of values and morality. I don't only speak from my personal perspective as a Christian but from the perspective of one watching the downgrading of humanity. For example, if people were honest and commercials in the media showed the effects of promiscuity the way some organizations now do with smoking, we would begin to see a change of behavior at some level. It seems like an insurmountable task, but if radio stations that play music promoting promiscuity would express the results of that promiscuity, that would have a real impact. It's hard to see that happening because then profits would be affected.

I would like to think that if given a choice, people would choose something else. If you always eat burgers, maybe gourmet salmon isn't your first choice. Your taste buds have been curved a certain way, and it will take training to sway them.

Back in 2006, there was an extremely popular song that came out; it was called *Promiscuous Girl*. It received rave reviews and awards and was being sung by kids all over the world, including those that were ignorant of the meaning of the word. The artist arrogantly and ignorantly promoted freedom of sexual expression to kids. The lyrics promoted sex with whomever they wanted at any particular time. I'm certain this irresponsible song caused the prolongation of STDs, unplanned pregnancy, and emotional repercussions beyond numeration for the millions that enjoyed its lyrics and message. It gave them validation in being a promiscuous boy or girl. The song, magnified by its popularity and influence, was a fad and disgrace.

Motivated by arrogance and greed, many musical artists spread their vulgarities and lyrical mis-messages and subsequently destroy lives. It has become increasingly popular to promote free casual sex through music and videos. Eighty to ninety percent of popular music videos shown on video networks promote free sex without restraint or commitment. Driven by profits and ratings, the network owners and show producers continue to air these videos and play these songs with little concern for the outcomes associated with their images and lyrics. The results we have seen are an explosion in the rate of sexually transmitted diseases.

The U.S. Centers for Disease Control and Prevention estimates that 19 million new STD infections occur each year. Among the most common STDs are chlamydia, gonorrhea, and syphilis, but the most common of all is the human papillomavirus (HPV) or genital warts. HPV can infect the mouth or the genitals, and most people do not know they are infected. HPV has been linked to cervical cancer, penile cancer, and both oral and throat cancers.

Having reached an epidemic proportion, HPV has caused a vaccination to be promoted to prevent the spread of this painful and incurable disease. HPV leads to other problems too. A study by the University of Texas Medical Branch has linked HPV to heart attack and stroke even when no typical cardiovascular health risks are present. It has become such a problem of epidemic proportions that now a vaccine is being pushed for it.

Commercials promote products that offer temporary relief to the blisters for Herpes sores or shots for chlamydia, syphilis, and gonorrhea infections. They fail to elaborate on or disclose the permanent damage these diseases cause, which includes sterility. I believe some people could be scared into avoiding some things if they actually rejected their arrogance and banished their ignorance.

It has been shown that HIV infections are increasing at alarming rates among some communities. It is painful to watch the decaying and wasting away of a people at an exponential rate. Nevertheless, arrogant, promiscuous people are willfully desensitized to the reality of HIV because of ignorance. They would rather not know they have it and risk spreading the disease than come off their selfish high horse and get tested. This should be a warning to those that engage in casual sex. The person you are having casual sex with would probably never expose the truth about their having HIV. So, if they do have the disease, you will find out when you get symptoms. The mere fact that a person is loose with sex should alert you that you are not the first one chosen to be his or her free sex partner.

Not everyone who becomes a victim is promiscuous, but great care should be taken. A firm commitment to openness and marriage are the greatest safeguards you can put in place to protect yourself. Buyer beware: it will cost you something, and it will probably be more than you're willing to pay. Emotionally or physically, you will have consequences for promiscuity and free sex. Free sex could eventually lead to the inability to have sex at all due to an eroded penis or a collapsed vagina because of disease. Looking at the pictures of that consequence online may cause some to have a change of heart about promiscuity.

This brings me to my final point. There has been an illusion painted and aimed directly at the public. The illusion is of safe sex outside of a monogamous husband and wife relationship. Here are some facts that can either be accepted or ignorantly rejected.

> Leakage of HIV particles occurs through condom holes in one-third of condoms. 1 in 3 condoms have holes and are leaking.

> The majority of STD's are initially asymptomatic. You may not know until it is too late. In other words, you may not know until you are scarred and before you have been to the doctor for medication.

> Viruses, including Herpes, HPV (warts), and HIV, are incurable. Other STDs leave irreversible damage that may not show up for years, even after treatment. When you want to have kids, you may not be able to because of damage.

> STD's can be transmitted through ALL sexual acts. For those knowledgeable to these facts, this may seem cliché, but my hope is that someone reading this will have an eye-opening revelation and change course before they arrive at a state of devastation.

I spent a previous chapter talking about the pregnancy factor of promiscuity, so I won't go into that again here. But, the issues associated with this, however, are a book in itself. They are frightening. The rise in sex trafficking and pornography addiction should also cause great alarm.

Concern for the safety of our children and hope of our future should cause conversation.

Hyper-sexuality of the culture is at an all-time high. Suburban husband and wives are running sex trafficking rings and performing unthinkable acts against the innocent. Increasingly, many in society sink into decadence and support outrageous and detrimental exposition through the media.

Promiscuity is a social ill that destroys people. It is usually rooted in ignorant arrogance of the consequences. Those that practice it are careless of the effects it has on their own and other people's psyche, body, and future. It is never too late to change course and start over, but it's always better to avoid the baggage in the first place.

A CHRISTIAN PERSPECTIVE

I remember a few years ago seeing a book titled *"Single and Having Sex."* The writer was discussing an issue that needed to be addressed among Christians. It would be naive to think that these issues are not a subject of discussion for Christians. Christians are always faced with decisions and choices related to sin. The laws that govern our behavior, however, must bring us to a place of godly submission, or the results will be the same among the Christian community as they are in the world.

The scripture *Psalms 119:11* gives us a foundational truth that can save us from so much heartache: *"Thy word have I hid in mine heart, that I might not sin against thee."* This scripture gives us an example of how to avoid sinning against God. This does not mean that we will get it right all the time. Thank God for many chances! However, the more we digest God's word and study His plan for successful and productive living, the more we will have positive outcomes in our lives. His Way is just a better way, and it saves us much time, hurt, and disappointment when we follow it.

There are many powerful and enlightening scriptures that we can review to see God's answers about promiscuity. These two passages below seem particularly pertinent.

Ephesians 5: 3: *"But sexual immorality and all impurity or covetousness must not even be named among you, as is proper among saints."*

I Corinthians 6: 9-10: *"Do you not know that the unrighteous and the wrongdoers will not inherit or have any share in the kingdom of God? Do not be deceived (misled): neither the impure and immoral, nor idolaters, nor adulterers, nor those who participate in homosexuality, nor cheats (swindlers and thieves), nor greedy graspers, nor drunkards, nor foulmouthed revilers and slanderers, nor extortioners and robbers will inherit or have any share in the kingdom of God."*

It is my intention to share the scripture as it is written by inspiration from God for correction, reproof, and training in righteousness according to the tenets in *II Timothy 3:16.*

Common sense would say that we should live in a way that avoids self-inflicted pain and trouble. The temptation to sin will always exist because the *Bible* says that sin is pleasurable. We, by nature, are pleasure-seeking. We must, however, die the mindset that causes us to seek pleasure above what we know is Christian reason, doctrine, and God's laws. Many are choosing to enjoy the pleasures of sin for a season, as outlined in *Hebrews 11:25*. These pleasures are seasonal, and the wages (payment) of sin is death.

The worldview is that people should seek out finding fulfillment through means that bring pleasure to our flesh. However, this fulfillment is short-lived and temporary. When we ground our fulfillment in spiritual things and things that please God, we have a gratification that lasts. People have sought to find this pleasure outside of God's will for relationships, and have been deceived by the media and others that ungodliness brings happiness. It is a counterfeit ideal. It is not God's plan for His children. The products of these relationships are not fruitful for living in God's best plan or design for His people. The enemy of our souls would have us to believe that there is an alternative to God's Way.

Our enemy's desire and role in the earth, according to scripture, is to steal, kill, and destroy; he enjoys destroying not only physically, but mentally. He has always tempted creation with things that contradict God's design in order to rebel against God. The fruit of this rebellion has always been separation from God and been detrimental to lives. We are given this example from the first man's fall in the garden because of the offer for an alternative lifestyle. God's Way is the only way that allows us real freedom and joy in life. Anything outside of His Will is counterproductive and destructive.

> ❝ *We will have to repent in this generation not merely for the vitriolic words and actions of the bad people but for the appalling silence of the good people. Martin Luther King, Jr.* ❞

BRAND
ARROGANCE

From Recording Artist to Business Executive, the value of a brand is determined by your fans or consumers. Unfortunately, the higher they rise, the more many lose sight of this basic fact. With humble beginnings, a recording artist begins a career while singing in small venues, local churches, or school programs. While receiving much praise and support, he or she perseveres through the myriad of talent and tribulation and rises to the occasion.

In time, those that have the "IT" factor find themselves in front of large crowds and cheering fans. Chart-topping songs, award-winning albums, and continuous media attention eventually become the norm and lose their initial impact and excitement. Then here comes the ugly head of arrogance. It is relentless.

The media with glee thrives on the ignorant arrogance of recording artists. It's expected, and in the typical interview, the questions are directed to elicit responses of self-praise. Being mostly subjective they create their own press. Eventually, many begin to feed into it and on it. This is not to say you shouldn't be self-confident and believe in your work. This unfortunately has to be moderated carefully as many go too far. Before you know it, artists are larger than life. Now fans have given them the perception that they will never leave them.

The harsh reality in today's short attention microwave society is that stars may not have that fame forever, at least not at the level needed to maintain the extravagance and excessiveness the life of a star demands. After all, fans expect and want artists to be living large if they are blowing them up into the stratosphere. In a fan's opinion, it is not okay for stars to be frugal or to live below their means. They want to see the excess. The expectation is that artists need to keep shining for them so that they can be proud to be a fan. No one asks any questions.

Years ago, it was revealed to one of the largest pop stars that she didn't have any money after her *tour*. After hearing rumors that she didn't have any money, she called to find out what people were talking about; to her surprise, she was broke in spite of her five #1 singles.

How could this be she asked? Her erratic decision to spend $3 million dollars on costumes had taken her over the edge. So, where was the business manager to stop her? Or could she not be stopped? Her response to this news was that she didn't care about money.

Here are a few examples of some of the biggest recording artists in history and their stories. They represent only a small percentage of the millions of stars that had their fifteen minutes or fifty years of fame and couldn't handle it.

*In 2007, things were starting to look up for "Un-break My Heart" singer Toni Braxton. Despite selling 25 million albums worldwide, she had declared bankruptcy in 1998 after racking up a $20,000 American Express bill and monthly expenses of over $43,000. However, she soldiered on with her career and released a popular new album in 2000, **The Heat**. Finally, she was back on track, and she could put her financial troubles behind her.*

Braxton's career renaissance was so successful that she was asked to headline the Flamingo Hotel in Las Vegas in 2006. The show proved so popular that its run was extended through 2008. However, in April of that year, she was hospitalized for chest pains, and as a heart disease sufferer, she decided not to further endanger her health. She decided to play it safe and cancel the remaining run of her show, but the cancellation incurred debts in the tens of millions of dollars. Braxton filed for bankruptcy a second time in October 2010. (Unknown, 2010)

Arrogance just won't let you see it all could be gone in a blink. So, ignorance triumphs.

MC Hammer *is fondly remembered for his hit songs, his energetic dancing, and his large billowy pants. He hit the big time in 1990 with the song "U Can't Touch This," and his album "Please Hammer Don't Hurt 'Em" went on to sell ten million copies. Hammer rewarded himself for his good fortune by buying a $30 million house and employing a full staff for it that cost him half a million dollars a month.Sadly, his fame didn't last, and before he knew it, he was $13.7 million in debt, with only $9.6 million in assets, prompting him to file for bankruptcy in 1996. Among the outstanding debts that he had at the time were $100,000 to the Internal Revenue Service, half a million dollars in legal fees, and another half a million dollars in the form of a loan from Deion Sanders of the Dallas Cowboys.* (Unknown, 2010)

The stories go on and on. Miscalculations and making bad investments, trusting the wrong advisors, and not keeping an eye on expenses top the downfall charts.

TO THE RECORDING ARTIST

One thing that should be remembered is that there is always someone coming up who could take your place, so take very good care to never arrive at the place called *there*. When you have *arrived*, you will begin to see your fall. The value you place on your brand is deceptive and not objective. Never believe your own press, as it is fleeting and will blow away with the wind when your hype runs out. In other words, people will love you today and move on tomorrow. If you're smart, you save up now, and you don't have to depend on their love to continue to thrive.

Please know that sometimes people come back around and love you again, sometimes more in death—Michael Jackson and Whitney Houston, for example. Whitney and Michael, some of the biggest stars of all time, were the focus of millions of negative blogs, posts, articles, tabloids, and news reports. Many of their fans helped perpetuate their demise through their slander, accusations, and abandonment. I imagine the weight of rejection by the millions who said they loved you can be pretty great.

That brings me to the brand arrogance of some of the great companies of the world. Growing up, I remember going to Blockbuster on the weekends and renting the latest blockbuster hit. It was a tradition and always exciting to pick out a movie. We would watch with friends and family and "make it a Blockbuster night." It never occurred to me that Blockbuster could ever go bust. It was a staple in most communities with brick and mortar stores on various corners and a place never to be undersold. So we thought.

So where did it all go so wrong? It started when arrogance caused Blockbuster to ignore the voice of their customers, the very ones who were keeping the doors open in the first place. I remember people always complaining. The late fees, poor customer service, and credit card requirements for membership were just a few of the things that drove their customers away. It seemed like the spirit of the company had a who-cares attitude. It was impossible to get much out of your in-store experience, and it ultimately ended up costing Blockbuster a lot.

Netflix came along and offered a better way to do business, and people responded. They gave us options, and many bought into it. The Blockbuster brand loyalty was a thing of the past, and we saw them slowly become irrelevant buildings that no one cared much to enter. Finally, I saw the results of their arrogance first hand. Signs in towns across America with the words, "Store Closing" appeared in Blockbusters. Week after week, the prices went down, and people came in and scavenged through the movies as the stores prepared to shut their doors.

Blockbuster, so confident in themselves, did too little, too late to make their customers feel valued and to move with the times. Now we see their competition following in those footsteps. It seems some can only learn by their own experience. Learning from the experience of others would diminish their arrogance. And after all, everyone feels what happened to others could never happen to you or to me. Yet, in spite of that feeling, brand arrogance will drive you to nothing really quick. The enormity of the list of those who can testify about this will never be known.

TO THE BUSINESS OWNER

Serve well. Your customers pay the bills and keep you in business. Creating a model within your business will cause this to be the tone of the brand and of its employees. Chick-Fil-A is a great example, in my opinion. The brand has developed a climate of people who make you feel welcome and are willing to serve.

I remember going into a franchise of this popular restaurant and having a spill from my then seven-year-old. It happens often, but I was hoping he could keep the lid on this time. Quickly, we had help with a warm smile from the management to clean up the mess. It left a great memory. It feels good to go to the drive-thru and get a nice smile and "How are you doing?" It's no wonder people supported this brand when it needed them.

A CHRISTIAN PERSPECTIVE

It's wonderful to know that the *Bible* has a remedy to all our troubles and issues. The following scripture is a good place to start when you need help. *"As for the rich in this present age, charge them not to be haughty, nor to set their hopes on the uncertainty of riches, but on God, who richly provides us with everything to enjoy. They are to do good, to be rich in good works, to be generous and ready to share, thus storing up treasure for themselves as a good foundation for the future, so that they may take hold of that which is truly life." 1 Timothy 6:17-19, ESV.*

This may be a hard set of rules to swallow. It is completely opposed to the normal course of things in the brands and artist agendas. I remember reading not long ago about one particular artist who had topped *Forbe's* list as the highest-paid artist. It was reported that the foundation to help kids that he had developed had been given $6 thousand from his earnings of $63 million dollars. Obviously, it really wasn't about the kids. The scripture from Timothy listed above would likely fall on deaf ears if told to that high-paid artist.

Churches and Christians are not exempt from their battle with brand arrogance. The rise of the mega-church and television evangelists has, in return, resulted in some of the largest scandals in Christian church history. The fame and glitz that go along with being on television and having a congregation of adoring members has gone to many heads. The scandalous behavior that can result from adulation and power is just an extension of arrogance. When secret deeds are exposed, and they still cannot be stopped, the feeling of invincibility causes some to go to extreme measures in an effort to keep that feeling in place and to stay on top.

The problem is not limited to those with their names in lights, however. Some of the smallest storefront ministries have fought their demons in public failure. Secret meetings with secretaries and under the table business transactions have tainted many ministries. Some have gone on to start denominations that practice strange rituals branding themselves with formal titles that make them feel more important. (i.e. Bishop, etc.). The role of being a servant just doesn't seem as attractive.

Likewise, Christian and gospel artists have fallen prey to the temptation to love praise more than humility. It doesn't seem to take much for them to give in at many levels to gain the acceptance of pop culture and mainstream media. False humility causes them to be self-deceived. They wish to portray the idea that they are Christ-motivated and that their actions are to promote the kingdom of Christ; however, soon enough, the absence of godly fruit exposes their real motivations.

Our example, Jesus Christ, came to demonstrate to us a model of servitude. The goal is to develop into the type of brand, personality, artist, or Average Joe who serves others. We see that modeled in scripture for us in *Ephesians 6-8* from the ESV: *"Rendering service with a good will as to the Lord and not to man, knowing that whatever good anyone does, this he will receive back from the Lord, whether he is a slave or free."*

It does not mean serving for the sake of a press release or television spot. It means serving as an example of Christ-likeness. If the things you are doing are simply self-promoting, you have gotten it all wrong. The motivation for doing good deeds should not be for what you can get out of it.

> *Arrogance diminishes wisdom*
> Arabian Proverb

> *When men are most sure and arrogant, they are commonly most mistaken, giving views to passion without that proper deliberation which alone can secure them from the grossest absurdities* David Hume

> *Everybody can be great because anybody can serve. You don't have to have a college degree to serve. You don't have to make your subject and verb agree to serve. You only need a heart full of grace. A soul generated by love.* Martin Luther King, Jr.

MARRIAGE WARS

This chapter, I hope, will be the most life-changing of any I have written so far. Marriage is defined as *the union between a man and a woman that is born out of a commitment to love and mutual respect.* The idea is that I'm better *with* you than *without* you. It may be troubling for some that have not been successful at marriage to read these words, but my hope is that you will see an opportunity to change some things and maybe have another chance.

When we go to the altar on that momentous day, we go with dreams, fantasies, ideas, and visions of magic. I remember my own wedding day as being somewhat of a fairy tale. It seemed surreal as I went through the motions of the ceremony and reception. It was a grand and beautiful occasion for me.

People start marriage as a journey to unite and find common ground, wherewith they will be able to have joy and peace in life. Then one day, in many cases, something happens to prompt one or both partners to question the dream. Arrogant rages and ignorant rants shake the foundations of the marriage, and some simply cave in and end.

Arrogance in marriage is one of the most damaging aspects of this powerful union. It may not be listed on the top ten reasons why people divorce, but arrogant roots lead to many sets of divorce papers.

Divorce results because someone just isn't happy with the way things are, and they decide that they want out. The question is, how much of your marriage was based on emotions and selfishness and how much was based on commitment and love? Abuse and adultery are not associated with any of the following statements I make in this chapter.

In recent times, we have seen a rise in the divorce rate to disheartening proportions. In a culture that is egotistic and driven by selfish pursuits, could not our rampant narcissism be a factor in the divorce epidemic? The newspaper ads for quick divorces have made it easy to get out of a situation where you are unfulfilled. For a few hundred dollars, maybe you could give it another shot and find someone who could really please you.

One of the characteristics of arrogance in a spouse is intolerance to differences of opinion. In other words, it's their way or no way at all. There is little room for discussion or reasoning. Storming out the rooms and screaming are forms of this type of arrogant temper tantrum spouse. There is no place for having a difference of opinion because as he or she sees it, only his or her way is the right perspective or point of view. Defensiveness is the response to any confrontation or correction, and anger ensues when anyone questions their reasoning or rationales. Unfortunately, before long, the opposing spouse feels it is impossible to remain in a situation where he or she is voiceless and disallowed the privilege of opinion. In more extreme cases, this arrogance escalates into violence.

So how does this translate into arrogance and not insecurity? It is actually a combination of both. The later is a root of arrogance. I will start with men to begin dissecting the root of this. Traditionally, men have been the head of the household in making the final decisions and governing their homes and families. Some, however, take this to the extreme because of insecurities. Instead of welcoming conversation to discuss important decisions, they believe they have all the answers, and there is no need for mutual contemplation on things.

When the wife begins to ask questions or voices an opinion, it becomes a war, and in this case, they will not back down. This type of arrogantly, ignorant man will see the deterioration of his family quickly. His insecurities become highlighted because he lacks the capability to want to learn. He would rather be ignorantly wrong than take the low road and admit it.

On the flip side, an arrogantly ignorant woman can have the same problem. Growing up in fatherless, women-directed homes, or being a successful career woman has caused many women to develop a overly dominant nature. Consequently, these women may lack the ability to allow their husbands to lead their households. Many women constantly belittle and disrespect their husbands without regard for their feelings. Their insecurities cause them to have the same response as arrogant men. The arrogant always need to be right and to have the upper hand in decision-making. Manipulation is one of the techniques these arrogant type of women use to hold their husbands hostage and to get what they want.

The marriages described become self-serving and no longer mutually beneficial. The bonds begin to unravel because the unity is lost, and things become one-sided. By no means am I saying this is the only reason people divorce, but I am saying it is a factor in many of them. When there is no sense of a partnership and concern for each other in a marriage, it dissolves even if the spouse doesn't leave.

The characteristics that keep marriages strong have to be developed in the early stages of the marriage. Ideally, weaknesses in these areas should be identified before marriage. Compromise is of great value in a healthy marriage. Finding a middle ground and learning to disagree and move on are key factors in making the marriage work. Both parties must be willing to take the low road for the sake of their love and commitment. It doesn't mean either one is right or wrong. It simply means they are moving on together.

Lack of appreciation and value is another trait of the arrogant spouse. This spouse finds it hard to celebrate or show appreciation for the other partner. It is a challenge to have attention diverted from them, so they fail to acknowledge or shower love and appreciation on the other mate unless there is a benefit to their ego or someone else is watching. The praise received from others for being a great husband or wife is the only incentive for these displays of affection. When no one is looking, attentiveness is no longer on the agenda.

These spouses arrogantly lose sight of reality and deceive themselves into believing they really *are* great spouses. After all, everyone is saying it and taking notice. They can shut it on and off like a water faucet and become masters of disguise when the time is right. Many of them show their true character later when the marriage fails by their own hand.

Arrogant spouses cause their spouses to feel as though they have no value. Frequent threats of leaving and finding someone better, put-downs, and inconsideration are characteristic. Verbal abuse in many of these instances causes the receiving spouse to have low self-esteem and to become withdrawn, which further enables the bullying spouse.

Another really big consideration in a strong marriage is the ability to say, 'I'm sorry." The problem with the arrogant spouse is that this would mean they have to admit they are wrong. The fact that they have convinced themselves that they are typically right would dispute this notion, and they just can't have that. Even when all the evidence points to error and wrongdoing, they find it *almost* more than they can do, if not absolutely impossible, to say the words that could change everything. They need to say, "I'm sorry."

The thing about saying, "I'm sorry," is that it causes you to evaluate yourself, to acknowledge that you have imperfections, and to accept that you are wrong. If you are full of insecurities that you have chosen not to accept nor change, it is much easier not to look at yourself as having the capacity for imperfections. The rose-colored glasses of peachy-keen existence feel so much better.

I find that others too have weighed in on the topics of marriage, relationship, and communication. Almost every authority agrees that:

It is arrogant for a spouse to think that his (or her) opinions are always the right ones. It is arrogant to think that there is no value in listening to others and opening up to new viewpoints and approaches. It is arrogant to put others down because they differ in how they think.

You are showing others your own limitations and insecurities if you demand that they admit you are right and they are wrong. "When you judge others, you do not define them; you define yourself," observed Earl Nightingale.

One of the marks of intelligence is to know what you do not know and to realize that there is always more to be learned. One of the marks of emotional maturity is to be able to admit when you are wrong, don't have all the answers, or need to apologize. It has been said that the five most essential words for a healthy, vital relationship are, "I apologize," and "You are right." (Wasson, N., 2006)

Adjustment to changes and finding balance are necessary steps in the preservation of a marriage. Being an unmovable rock that is unwilling to bend and adjust to circumstances because of ego and narcissism will end a marriage quickly. Many individuals living in arrogance move on to another marriage, because in ignorance, after all, *they* couldn't see anything wrong with themselves, so what went wrong must have been with the other person. The fact that their spouse could not cater to all their needs and egotistic desires, will drive them away or into the arms of another in search of someone to make them feel bigger and better about themselves.

The next spouse or relationship should beware. Most likely, the insufficiency in the other person's ability to keep them feeling and looking good will push demanding spouses to similar results unless they put an end to their arrogance and change. Marriage is a beautiful thing, but arrogance can turn it into a living hell. The effects not only affect the other spouse, but they spill over to the children involved. They see the tumultuous roller-coaster relationship and develop similar patterns and mindsets that they will carry over into their own relationships. It is important to model wholesomeness to children lest you create a generational cycle of dysfunction. Fathers and mothers should model temperance and patience, demonstrate compromise and appreciation, and show a willingness to apologize. These key elements make for a happy home.

The lives the arrogant spouse damages are far-reaching. Friendships, families, and communities have suffered because they just couldn't extend themselves enough to care about someone else due to the size of their ego and the extent of their self-centeredness. What an arrogant spouse has felt in a moment, has caused many of them to make decisions that have hurt people for a lifetime. The trail of pain and problems that result sometimes never see recovery. The rise in the lack of empathy discussed in a previous chapter has caused people to be less concerned about the effects of their behavior and decisions on others. The rise in self-empowerment books that promote living your best life, etc. has harmed many people by inadvertently condoning the irrationality behind selfish decisions.

Happiness is a mood that can change in a moment. However, it has become a determining factor in decisions that involve commitment, integrity, and empathy. Rushing to make decisions based on the gauge of happiness involved has caused extensive loss and brought pain to countless millions. Arrogance is stubborn, too; it didn't allow that husband or wife to turn back after walking out the door, even though this may have been exactly the right thing to do.

The sooner husbands and wives see that the world does not revolve around them and truly learn to love and appreciate someone else, the better the world will be. How can you be a loving and giving spouse when you are consumed with low-esteem and misery? Accepting your individual flaws and failures and admitting the need to take another course are key.

A marriage born out of arrogance and not humility will always be in a fight for survival until real humility takes over. Marriage commitment and vows cannot be based on changeable feelings, but on a solid foundation of love. Love is a choice; it goes beyond feelings that may shift from day to day. Expectations should be based on a commitment to work together, to demonstrate love, and to give mutual respect.

Some marriages simply won't work because violence and self-centeredness will not be abandoned. The results: infidelity, abuse, rage, and inconsistency. Ultimately, divorce ensues when there is no commitment to positive needed change. Marriage is a work in progress, and the determination to conquer problems and to build a future is essential to the marriage's success.

A CHRISTIAN PERSPECTIVE

Marriage is honorable between a man and a woman. God blesses the union that is ordained by Him. God commands men to love their wives, wives to submit to their husbands, as well as mutual submission to each other. The command does not notate submission in a negative context but in a positive connotation.

In the current thinking of modern culture, because of ignorance, this premise has been attacked as outdated. In other words, wives should humble themselves in dealing with their husbands. Likewise, husbands should love their wives. This would make it necessary for husbands to humble themselves to demonstrate love in their actions and dealings with their wives. Love *is* an action and a *decision* that is made daily. I didn't say it was easy, but it is worth the fight.

The scripture I love on this topic is, "*Whoso findeth a wife findeth a good thing, and obtaineth favour of the LORD.*" *Proverbs 18:22.* The intention God has is that a man finds his wife and not vice versa. When a man does find a wife or choose a wife, he finds something that is good and pleasurable. Be careful that you are looking deeper than the surface. What he does with that is up to him. If he chooses well, he will obtain favor from the Lord. Favor can take you very far. *Proverbs 31:23* says that a man is known in the gates (of the city) because of his wife. She brings a good reputation to him and doesn't bring harm to his name or brand.

Why do you think politicians have their wives to speak during their campaigning? People tend to look at the wife to form opinions about the husband; this is true even in politics. Men these days should not seek out wives based on television standards but should look for a woman that is pleasing to the Lord. This is a pivotal first step toward a healthy marriage. We see God's plan for marriage to be a union in Mark 10:6-9: *"But at the beginning of creation God 'made them male and female. For this reason, a man will leave his father and mother and be united to his wife, and the two will become one flesh. So they are no longer two, but one. Therefore what God has joined together, let man not separate."*

> *Many marriages would be better if the husband and the wife clearly understood that they are on the same side.* Zig Ziglar

> *It is not a lack of love, but a lack of friendship that makes unhappy marriages.* Friedrich Nietzsche

> *Marriage: Love is the reason. Lifelong friendship is the gift. Kindness is the cause. Till death do us part is the length.* Fawn Weaver

> *The most desired gift of love is not diamonds or roses or chocolate. It is focused attention.* Rick Warren

HAPPINESS IN HUMILITY

Nearing the close of this book I wanted to present you with a summation of my personal philosophy.

I didn't come from humble beginnings, and by many estimations I was born into privilege and blessing. This by default can cause an elevated sense of entitlement in life and being.

On the flipside, those that are born in struggle and disdain have an inner fight as well. It can create people with superficial and fabricated personas who are desperate to show their rise to prominence and importance, often in an extremely inflated way.

Humility causes you to see your inefficiencies and short coming and to accept your need for correction or assistance in changing things that bring trouble to your life.

To live in contentment while pursuing dreams and goals and not compromise integrity for self gratification; to seek to give yourself to others without the need for praise or applause are the tenets of those seeking a path of humility. Happiness and ultimate wholeness can be found in humility. The pursuit of it never ends.

ways to control the and the pursuit of it never ends. The rewards of its acquisition, however, at each stage in life's journey are joy and fulfillment.

So how do we find balance and resolution to our fallen nature? I live by the quote, "humble yourself or you will be humbled by force." As I have attempted to show throughout the course of these writings, no good comes out of haughtiness. Frankly, I think it impossible to fully attain a grounded life without a revelation beyond your natural abilities.

As a Christian, my foundation is built in the teachings of the *Bible*, where the greatest example of humility was Jesus Christ. It is with daily pursuit that I must fight the temptation to rise above my capabilities and realize that I am not God. It is with sincerity that I tell you that I am desperately in need of a Savior and enlightenment beyond mundane human experience to overcome one of the greatest human challenges of all—humility.

No matter what you believe, whether you are an atheist, an agnostic, or a believer, failure or survival in life will be connected to your state of humility. Characteristics of the humble or those works in progress striving for humility are:

- Willingness to love someone without reciprocation
- Responsibly guarding your actions and attitudes for the sake of others
- Accepting the challenge of being wrong and receiving answers
- Welcoming the tests of humility

All these attributes, which may not be innate, build character; a character that fights arrogance, so that you can be productive and develop into a balanced individual. Society may have gotten off track, but the more we reject ignorance, kill arrogance, and embrace humility, the better off the world is every day.

It would be arrogant for people, after reading this book, to suggest that none of this applies to them and that they have completely mastered this life's excursions. I envision the effect of this book to be that everyone who reads it can gain some sense of redirection from it...as I have myself while writing it.

> *Do you wish to rise? Begin by descending. You plan a tower that will pierce the clouds? Lay first the foundation of humility.*
> <u>Saint Augustine</u>

> *Fullness of knowledge always means some understanding of the depths of our ignorance; and that is always conducive to humility and reverence.* <u>Robert Millikan</u>

> *So much of how we act and what we do is based on humility or pride—that's everything. And when you can humble yourself, you know, we are more like Christ when we can humble ourselves.* <u>Tim Tebow</u>

> *Whoever exalts himself with haughtiness and empty pride shall be humbled (brought low), and whoever humbles himself whoever has a modest opinion of himself and behaves accordingly shall be raised to honor.* Mathew 23: 12

8 Things You Can Do To Reverse the Tendency to Arrogance

Smile. A smile can open up the world. Walking around with a frown all day shows the world you just aren't that interested in anyone around you. Your frown makes people uncomfortable

Listen. It is such a pain having a conversation with someone who can't shut up. They only want to hear what *they* have to say. Learn to care about what someone else has to say enough to just listen.   Sharing what you did last summer, may cost you a golden nugget toward your future.

Kindness. Random acts of kindness may seem insignificant, but it humbles you. It takes you out of what you need and gives to someone else. It brightens someone's day. Put yourself in someone else's shoes.

Speak to people with respect and gentleness.

Stop being rude and moody. A soft answer turns away wrath. You can catch more bees with honey than with vinegar.

Read. It will show you that you have so much more to learn and that you really can't be a know it all.

Go to lunch and make friends. It helps you learn to enjoy other people and what they contribute to the world.

Be grateful and say it often. Thank God throughout the day, and count your many blessings. It reminds you that there is Someone greater than you making things happen.

THE GREATEST
OF ALL

For centuries, mortal man has debated and disputed the case of immortality and the supernatural. There has been scientific research, and great lengths have been taken to disprove the existence of God and forces outside of our natural experience. Until recent times, there has been limited science to back up the claims of spiritual leaders and theologians. Determinedly, many held to their ignorant theories and mindsets without wavering.

Could man be so ignorant and arrogant to believe that everything we see manifested on the Earth was not the work of a supernatural ability and far beyond our limited capacity? How could it be denied that it was nothing less than the handy work of a supreme being beyond the comprehension of our finite understanding? We need only look at the function of microscopic cells that miraculously come together to intrinsically form a web of DNA that produces human life. Or can we overlook the seed that, when planted in the ground, divinely interacts with soil and water to produce trees that release oxygen for life cycles to continue? Is this not the work of Someone greater than our comprehension? How can it be denied?

However, it still remains true that those who expend all their energy to develop theories attempt to explain away the divine. In pure arrogance, many have sought to disprove the laws of nature, albeit divine nature beyond human thought capacity. This is frivolous, futile, and the greatest waste of time there is.

In recent times, man has gone to great extremes to have his way within the laws of nature and natural existence. There is no sensible debate on this matter. There is no disputing the natural order of things. Science and biology should be enough to back this up, but this has proven not to be for some. Can we humanly redefine or change the natural function of a thing? Can we now say a tree's function is not to produce shade, oxygen, and timber, because it no longer suits our arrogant agendas? It is ignorant and a sign of the times.

God, in His infinite wisdom, set things in order to cause the earth to be fruitful and function properly in His ideal design. When the natural order of things is disrupted, the results are chaos, dysfunction, and deformity. The by-product of man's arrogant ego is failure. We will never stand against God and win.

Sin will never be legitimately justified, no matter how many counterfeit theories come into play. The results will never be authentic or true. It is a great deception in the earth that has caused the drastic rise in distorted thinking and arrogant manifestations of this thinking. The consequences of human attempts to usurp God's Will and ordering of things will always result in destruction. Man's ignorance of God's supremacy predicates living in open rebellion to His ways and a rejection of His purpose. God's response to rebellion is His wrath after His mercy is rejected.

It is not my intention to ever debate this subject concerning the lawfulness of sin, because it is just plain ignorant to waste time in this conversation. Those that are not spiritual will never understand spiritual things. *Titus 3: 9- 11* admonishes us to avoid vain arguments because they are unfruitful. If people don't want to receive the truth after it is extended, they must simply be left alone.

We must, by our Christian position, present the truth for their consideration, but one's will can never be overturned without consent. It is his or her heart's decision that God will ultimately look at and judge. Our knowledge of truth is a position of faith that cannot be placed on anyone without their making choices to accept it. This is a decision that is made in faith to believe God's word and to practice His ordinances the way He designed them and set them in order.

Rejects and rebels of God will always find rationales for a distorted and corrupt mindset in matters of sinfulness that they want to justify or find excuses to participate in. Sin is pleasurable for a season, so people find reasons to indulge in it. However, the wages of sin is death. I have never seen a life of practicing sin not cause destruction in some area.

I have often heard people say that the world is getting worse. People have been repeating the same mistakes forever. No matter how many examples they see, people will never change until they receive the Great Hope.

> **"**
>
> *The world's corruption is a result of its defiance.*
> Warren Wiersbe
>
> **"**

> **"**
>
> *For there is no one so great or mighty that he can avoid the misery that will rise up against him when he resists and strives against God.* John Calvin
>
> **"**

OUR ONLY HOPE

The first sin of mankind was arrogance. In arrogant rebellion and ignorant understanding, the first man's testing of wills overstepped his boundaries, and Adam disobeyed God's order. The result was the curse of sin-nature. The only hope for salvation from this nature is redemption received through Jesus Christ.

As a Christian, it is easy to say we have received this grace and to deny struggling with our nature. However, in our process of sanctification, it is a daily dying of wills and desires that produces the Christ-like nature in us. Christ-like nature seeks to kill arrogance at the very inclination of its uprising.

We can only do this by God's power. It is not within our own strength that we can put to rest this propensity to rebel against God. It is in our DNA to have dominance on earth. Man was given a degree of dominion in the universe but was also given boundaries. The boundaries of our existence must not be crossed. Those boundaries are God's laws, precepts, and ways. If and when we cross them, we must be corrected or chastised for our own good. God's laws are put in place for our protection and preservation.

Man falls and disintegrates when he is out of place with God.

The question is how to live in joy, peace, and contentment in a world pressuring us to be discontented. In other words, there is no fulfillment in the world system. There is always a striving for more gain or satisfaction. There is an unquenchable thirst for power, things, status; all rooted in arrogant pursuit. It is, however, all done in ignorance.

The source of all sustainable pleasure is ultimately found in God's Will and presence. Every effort to fill the void God designed will result in dissatisfaction.

As the world draws farther away from a pursuit of God and His favor, we see the rise in depression, suicide, loneliness, perversion, and wickedness. Avocations toward pleasure and happiness apart from the desires of God result in desperate failure. Temporary highs don't last, and the hole of emptiness expands with each attempt at filling it. We have seen this in examples of those whose lives are in the spotlight. More money, more fame, more status, more applause, more admiration, and still, there is no hope.

Christians are not exempt from losing faith. As we fall away from the grace and hope that brought us to peace, we will see results no different than those that have never experienced the hope we have. God, however, will draw us back by extreme measures if necessary. Earnestly and passionately maintaining your place in God's law willingly, is much more desirous and easier than the alternatives.

God will not share His Glory or His space with anyone or anything. I have heard it said that He is passionate for His glory. The plight of humanity is to settle down and accept this truth. It cannot be overturned by any effort of man. He will, by any means, get His glory. *Romans 14: 11*, is clear on this: "*Every knee shall bow and every tongue shall confess to God.*" Whether you do it now or later, it shall be done.

God will not share His Glory or His space with anyone or anything. I have heard it said that He is passionate for His glory. The plight of humanity is to settle down and accept this truth. It cannot be overturned by any effort of man. He will, by any means, get His glory. Romans 14: 11, is clear on this: "Every knee shall bow and every tongue shall confess to God." Whether you do it now or later, it shall be done.

> *Self-seeking is the gate by which a soul departs from peace; and total abandonment to the will of God, that is by which it returns.* Madame Guyon

BIBLIOGRAPHY

Bartlett, John. (1992). Bartlett's familiar quotations: A collection of passages, phrases, and proverbs traced to their sources in ancient and modern literature. New York: Little Brown.

Brennan, Christine. (April 16, 2012.) Entitlement and Epidemic in Sports. USA TODAY.

Crossway Bibles. (2008). The esv study bible. Wheaton, IL: Crossway Bibles.

Gibbs, Nancy. (May 19, 2011). Sex, lies, arrogance: what makes powerful men behave so badly? Retrieved from

http://www.time.com/time/magazine/article/0,9171,2072641,00.html#ixzz22PU71NcG

Gray, Thomas. (2011). An elegy in a country churchyard: and ode on a distant prospect of eton college. Charleston, SC: Nabu Press.

Karim, Reef. (December 19, 2009). The reality tv obsession: A psychological study. Retrieved from

http://sobertransitions.typepad.com/sobertransitions/2009/12/the-reality-tv-obsession-a-psychological-investigation.html

Karwacki, Francis. (January 2012). Texting creates an artificial world. Retrieved: from

http://newsitem.com/opinion/letters/texting-creates-an-artificial-world-1.1317253 "reprinted with permission."

Knufken, Drea. (1 January, 2009). 25 athletes who went broke. Retrieved October 18, 2011 from

http://www.businesspundit.com/25-rich-athletes-who-went-broke-10-1"reprinted with permission."

Lytton, Edward Bulwer. (1989). Zanoni: A rosicrucian tale. Herndon, VA: Steinerbooks.

Mcgraft, Jane. (2012). Top 5 white-collar crimes. Retrieved from

http://investigation.discovery.com/top-ten/white-collar-crimes/famous-white-collar-crimes.html

Muehlenberg, Bill.(Oct.18,2010).Why children need a mother and a father. Retrieved from

http://www.billmuehlenberg.com/2010/10/18/why-children-need-a-mother-and-a-father/

NAMA. (April 1, 2011) Study shows saggy pants linked erectile dysfunction & other health issues. Retrieved from

http://hiphopandpolitics.wordpress.com/2011/04/01/study-shows-saggy-pants-linked-erectile-dsyfunction-other-health-issues/

O'Connor, James (July 9, 2012). Facing the world. Retrieved from

http://www.cusscontrol.com

Perri, Frank. (Spring 2008). The arrogant chameleons: Exposing fraud-detection homicide. Retrieved from

http://www.all-about-psychology.com/support-files/exposing_fraud_detection_homicide.pdf

Peterson, Eugene H.(n.d.). The message from Matthew 13-16. Retrieved from

http://www.biblegateway.com/passage/?search=Matthew%20 5:13-16&version=MSG

Rhodes, Codi. (August 21, 2011). For some reality tv stars, turmoil follows fame. Retrieved from

http://www.13wmaz.com/life/entertainment/article/140851/18/For-Some-Reality-TV-Stars-Turmoil-Follows-Fame-

Small, Gray & Vorgan, Gigi. (February 18, 2011). Is the internet killing empathy? Retrieved from

http://articles.cnn.com/2011-02-18/opinion/small.vorgan.internet. empathy_1_brains-fatal-car-crash-facebook-friends?_s=PM:OPINION

Staehle, Dori. (Feb. 15, 2012). Casting a wider net: Why colleges are recruiting homeschoolers. Retrieved from

http://www.nextstage-edu.com/2012/02/15/casting-a-wider-net-why-colleges-are-recruiting-homeschoolers/

Tardanico, Susan. (April 30, 2012). Is social media sabotaging real communication? Retrieved from

http://www.forbes.com/sites/susantardanico/2012/04/30/is-social-media-sabotaging-real-communication/.

Tat, Jennifer. (Nov. 9, 2010) When cyberbullying turns deadly. Retrieved from

http://www.dailytitan.com/2010/11/cyber-bullying/

Tillman, Jodie. (March 15, 2011). Sagging pants' bill passes house committee. Retrieved from

http://www.tampabay.com/blogs/the-buzz-florida-politics/content/sagging-pants-bill-passes-house-committee

Torre, Pablo S. (2009). How (and why) athletes go broke. Retrieved from

http://sportsillustrated.cnn.com/vault/article/magazine/MAG1153364/1/index.htm

Unknown, (Nov 29, 2010). Famous musicians who had it all and ended up in bankruptcy. Retrieved from

http://www.mediadump.com/hosted-id106-famous-musicians-who-had-it-all-and-ended-up-in-bankruptcy.html

Unknown. (March 2010). Ten celebrities who went broke. Retrieved from

http://www.kzsq.com/2010/03/10-celebrities-who-went-broke

Unknown. (n.d.). Arrogance definitions. Retrieved from

http://en.wiktionary.org/wiki/arrogance.

Unknown. (n.d.). The Maury Povich show. Retrieved from

http://www.nationmaster.com/encyclopedia/The-Maury-Povich-Show
Unknown.(n.d.). Reality TV description in Wikipedia. Retrieved from

http://en.wikipedia.org/wiki/Reality_tv

Wasson, Nancy. (March 8, 2006). Why always having to be right can poison
your marriage. Retrieved from

http://ezinearticles.com/?Why-Always-Having-to-Be-Right-Can-Poison-
Your-Marriage&id=158517

Zondervan. (2011). Amplified Bible. Nashville, TN: Zondervan.

Made in the USA
Las Vegas, NV
23 April 2021

21866164R00079